Table of Contents

Table of Contents

Introduction

Peace. Calm. Rest.

If we're honest, these words probably don't describe our lives as much as we wish. Maybe they don't describe your life at all ... ever.

With so much that fights for our focus, it's hard to keep our eyes on God. And with so much that makes our hearts race, our eyes wander and our minds scatter, it seems impossible to keep anxiety, worry and stress from taking up permanent residence.

Yet God, through Paul in the book of Philippians, calls us to *"not be anxious about anything,"* and tells us that *"the peace of God, which transcends all understanding, will guard your hearts and your minds in Christ Jesus"* (Philippians 4:6-7).

How can that be, when the to-do list keeps growing?
When you are rejected or overlooked?
When you lose your job, the doctor calls with bad news, or you can't seem to fight off the loneliness any longer?
When you've prayed and prayed, but God seems to have His phone on Do Not Disturb?

The answer is found in Philippians 4:4-7:

> **"Rejoice in the Lord always. I will say it again: Rejoice! ... The Lord is near.**
>
> **Do not be anxious about anything, but in every situation, by prayer and petition, with**
>
> **thanksgiving, present your requests to God. And the peace of God, which transcends**
>
> **all understanding, will guard your hearts and your minds in Christ Jesus."**

When we keep our focus on God and who He is, our anxiety, worry and stress take a backseat to His peace, presence and promises.

It's hard to focus on our worries when we *"rejoice in the Lord."* It's difficult to feel overwhelmed with anxiety when we take hold of the truth that *"The Lord is near."* And it's impossible to be ruled by stress when we sit at His feet to *"present [our] requests ... with thanksgiving."*

This book is designed to bring your focus back to who God is: trustworthy, faithful and our defender. These comforting and uplifting devotions were written by members of COMPEL Training, Proverbs 31 Ministries' online writer training program, and are divided into sections based on the characteristics of God.

At the end of each devotion is the phrase, "God's reassurance for me is ..." In the lines underneath, write how God speaks to you through His Word and that day's devotion. What reassurance does He give that speaks to your current situation or worry? These sections will be beautiful reminders when you're feeling unsteady in the future and need reminding of His past faithfulness.

It's so easy to feel alone in our personal struggles. We wonder if anyone's ever felt the way we feel. We pray that through these devotions, you will feel less alone. You will know there are fellow believers who not only understand, but have experienced hope that is available to you.

We pray this book encourages you to fix your eyes on Jesus (Hebrews 12:2) — and ultimately to experience more of Him, His peace and His love.

GOD IS

TRUSTWORTHY

FREEING MY HEART FROM THE PRISON OF WORRY

SHIRLEY DESMOND JACKSON

"But store up for yourselves treasures in heaven, where moths and vermin do not destroy, and where thieves do not break in and steal. For where your treasure is, there your heart will be also."
Matthew 6:20-21 (NIV)

Sighing, I peered at the clock. Even before my alarm announced the day, an all-too-familiar sense of impending doom enveloped my spirit. Not ready to begin my morning, yet unable to fall back asleep, I wearily pulled myself out of bed.

Focus, I reminded myself. Remember to focus.

My battle with anxiety began as a young child. Whenever I fear failure, or my life begins to spin out of control, stress steals my peace and kills my joy. Worry loves to take my heart hostage.

On this particular morning, three equally distressing events set the stage for anxiety to capture my heart and create chaos:

An aging parent's health began to fail.
An adult child made a painful choice.
A work environment suddenly turned hostile.

Any one of these situations would have caused angst, but the combination threatened to completely crush me. My heavy heart struggled to find peace as my thoughts exploded in a thousand different directions. Unanswerable questions of "what if …" flooded my consciousness.

What do we do when the world shatters around us, making us feel powerless and without hope? How can we restore peace to our hearts?

Jesus teaches us we need to focus:

"But store up for yourselves treasures in heaven, where moths and vermin do not destroy, and where thieves do not break in and steal. For where your treasure is, there your heart will be also" (Matthew 6:20-21).

In this passage, Jesus uses the word "treasure" figuratively. Translated as a storehouse of riches, it includes the treasured thoughts we store up in our hearts and minds. Jesus promises our hearts will follow wherever we put our treasure.

This means I can determine the condition of my heart simply by choosing where I store my treasure. It really does come down to focus.

The Apostle Paul mirrored this message when he reminded us to "*[fix] our eyes on Jesus*" (Hebrews 12:2). In order to fix our eyes on Jesus, we must turn them away from everything else. So when anxiety presses in and fills my heart with wild, unsettling thoughts, I have a choice. Where will I place my treasure?

If I focus on uncertainty and allow my thoughts to run rampant, my heart will remain worry's prisoner. But I have another option. I can focus on Jesus.

Fixing my eyes on Jesus will not cure my mother, shield my child from the consequences of a bad decision, or restore harmony to my workplace. But when I dive into my treasury of Jesus, I find these precious gems:

A light to pierce my darkness. (John 8:12)
A shepherd to guide my path. (John 10:14)
A partner to lighten my load. (Matthew 11:29-30)

As I focused on Jesus that morning, my heart finally found its place, nestled in Jesus, my treasure. Finally ready to face my day, I stepped out, not with dread, but determination.

With Jesus as my treasure, anxiety no longer holds my heart captive.

God's reassurance for me is ...

CALM ASSURANCE IN A HEATED MOMENT

MISTY MCELROY

"When they hurled their insults at him, he did not retaliate; when he suffered,
he made no threats. Instead he entrusted himself to him who judges justly."
1 Peter 2:23 (NIV)

It was Monday morning, and at least one hard conversation waited for me at the office. I tried to mentally prepare, gripping the steering wheel as I switched lanes on the familiar, three-mile bridge that had carried me through years of weekday commutes.

Under a bright blue sky, early sunlight scattered diamonds on the river below, but inside, I couldn't shake the uneasy knot that formed in the pit of my stomach.

The customer in question was termed an "abusive caller," someone who had already hurled insults and veiled threats at me and others on my team. It was up to me to call him back with a resolution, but after our last conversation on Friday, I knew the exchange wouldn't be pretty.

For years, I've tried to fight my own battles in the face of adversity, especially when the stress of heated moments brings me to the breaking point. This escalated complaint was no exception.

Later that morning on the call, I adjusted my headset as I heard the expected onslaught of ugly words, ill wishes and unfounded slander. The all-too-familiar strain on my emotions threatened to make a bad situation worse.

I wanted to strike back. I wanted to defend my team and the actions of our company. But the words of 1 Peter 2:23 stopped me: *"When they hurled their insults at him, he did not retaliate; when he suffered, he made no threats. Instead he entrusted himself to him who judges justly."*

I pressed mute for just a moment, let out a long, low breath and offered a silent prayer. There might not be a way out, but there is a way through.

When life spins out of control, it's tempting to leverage the power of human strength, and Peter knew firsthand the inner turmoil of wanting to handle things on his own. While he didn't always choose the challenges that came his way, he did try to manipulate the outcome of some.

In a heated, historic moment, Peter witnessed the ultimate betrayal of Christ in the Garden of Gethsemane, and then Peter drew a sword and struck the servant of the high priest. Years later, perhaps this memory was etched into Peter's heart. Like gold refined, perhaps the fire of such a trial tempered Peter in a way that compelled him to share this message with future generations.

He watched Christ walk *through* when He wanted to walk *out*. He watched Him suffer without seeking revenge and surrender His own will when it would have been much easier to use strength or force.

On that uncertain Monday morning at work, I wasn't able to provide the desired outcome, but I was able to surrender the battle and acknowledge the pain on the other side of the line without giving in to the pressure of a heated debate. The customer and I came to agreeable terms, and as time continues, I'm learning that problem resolution isn't always as much about the outcome as it is about whether or not I'm Christlike during the process.

In Christ, we have an advocate who cares, and ever so gently, He beckons us to do the same. Above the turmoil. Beyond the pain. He offers a tender invitation to respond, lay each burden down and trust in the power of His name.

I don't know what battle or challenge you face today, but when hard conversations show up on the calendar or carefully laid plans take an unexpected turn, there is calm assurance in remembering Christ paved the way before us. In turn, He now also invites us to look up and trust Him who judges justly for comfort, peace and strength in the middle of life's heated moments.

God's reassurance for me is ...

GOD PAYS IN FULL

SHIRLEY MOORE

"Before they call, I will answer; while they are still speaking, I will hear."
Isaiah 65:24 (NIV)

Self-employment can be like a roller coaster. For us, it was no different. Very young, and with three preschool-age children, my husband and I started a small manufacturing business with borrowed equipment and one week's paycheck. It was sink or swim, and swim we did. Eighty-hour work weeks and financial hurdles were common.

In September 1992, we encountered considerable unexpected expenses during a transition. We could meet our obligations if — and only if — every one of our clients fully paid his or her statement that month. Therein was the problem. We had a particular client who never paid his monthly statement in full. Never. Not one time in the prior seven years.

Doubtful and anxious one afternoon, I sought the Lord. I acknowledged to God that He was sovereign and knew our needs before the foundation of the world. I declared to Him (and myself) that He promised to supply all of our needs according to His riches in glory by Christ Jesus. (Philippians 4:19) I confessed that I would trust in His promise that *"we know that all things work together for good to those who love God ..."* (Romans 8:28).

Whatever came — or didn't come — He would see us through. Focusing on God's powerful promises helped harness my racing mind from brooding over impulsive ways to try to fix our situation.

That same day, our particular client's payment arrived. For the first time in seven years, he paid 100% of his monthly statement rather than carry a balance. Coincidence? Not likely. For more than a decade thereafter, he never again paid his monthly statement amount in full.

Because that check was on its way days before my prayer, I pondered Isaiah 65:24, where God declares: *"It shall come to pass that before they call, I will answer, and while they are still speaking, I will hear."* The prophetic Scripture in Isaiah refers to events yet to come, but God does not change. (Malachi 3:6) Nor does His Son, Jesus, who *"is the same yesterday, today, and forever"* (Hebrews 13:8). God has heard His children and met their needs through the ages. He does today. He will tomorrow.

Oftentimes, answers do not come quickly, and sometimes the outcome is not what we desired. But God used the timing of the check's arrival to reinforce in me that He is in control, cares for us and is working all things for good for those who love Him. It was a faith builder. He has proven faithful time and again through much larger challenges and loss due to illness or death.

Truly, we overcome anxiety when we pray with thanksgiving and present our requests to God. (Philippians 4:6) Cast your cares on Him because He cares for you. (1 Peter 5:7) Focusing on God's promises and power forces our fear to submit to faith in our Savior.

God's reassurance for me is ...

A STEADFAST MIND

CARLY SPENCE

"You keep him in perfect peace whose mind is stayed on you, because he trusts in you.
Trust in the LORD forever, for the LORD GOD is an everlasting rock."
Isaiah 26:3-4 (ESV)

The early morning sun streamed through my bedroom window, pulling me awake far sooner than I would have wished. I sighed heavily and glared at my clock before flopping onto my back. I sighed again as I contemplated the day before me, the silence of my apartment further darkening my mood. Another long, empty Saturday had begun.

I was entering my second decade of singleness and there were many days when I longed for companionship. That's not to say that I didn't have friends and family, but I still found myself alone far more often than I would've liked. And when you're frequently alone, it's easy to get lost in a downward spiral of tangled thoughts: *Why don't I have more friends? No one really likes you, you know. I always feel so rejected.* On and on the insecurity and lies would go, until I dreaded the days and weeks ahead.

God's Word, however, is the beautiful antidote to all of the dark thoughts that can sicken our souls. I love Isaiah 26:3 and go to it often: *"You keep him in perfect peace whose mind is stayed on you ..."* Other translations incorporate the word "steadfast," which means "firmly fixed, immoveable, not subject to change." We don't have to wander around in the darkness of insecurity, anxiety and rejection. Those thoughts are from the devil, and they are not true! Instead, we can fix our minds firmly on the truth of the Lord, who, according to verse 4, is our everlasting rock.

Having a steadfast mind is not something that happens by accident. I have had to work hard to block out the negative thoughts and influences that want to race around unchecked in my brain. In order to be at peace and resting on God's truth, I need to read His Word, meditate on His message and pray for His help daily. His words will begin to take up residence in my mind and start to push the dark thoughts away. Through His power, I can learn to trust in the everlasting rock and keep my mind steadfast.

I can receive my gift of singleness with gratitude and joy.
I can look to Him for direction in my daily life.
I can give my extra time back to Him as an offering.
I can remember that it is God alone who gives my life purpose.

It is not easy to hold on to these truths. There are many days when I still struggle to keep my mind on God, but He is faithful. If you feel discouraged about the days ahead, I want to challenge you to fill your mind with Scripture. Prepare yourself to be steadfast and trust the Lord to be the only true source of peace in your life.

God's reassurance for me is ...

WHAT IF?

STEVEN DIIOIA

"Then an angel from heaven appeared and strengthened him. He prayed more fervently, and he was in such agony of spirit that his sweat fell to the ground like great drops of blood."
Luke 22:43-44 (NLT)

The "what if" anxiety alarm continues to blare in my mind ... *What if _____ happens? What if ___ doesn't happen? What if nothing happens?* Each "what if" adds to the load I am already carrying.

I am a believer, so it isn't right to feel this way ... is it? God tells me to hand my burdens to Him, but *what if* He doesn't handle them quickly enough? What if He doesn't handle them the way I *want* them to be handled?

Wrestling with my faith drains my strength, making it harder to turn to God, especially when my focus is on the storm around me. What if God tells me, "Don't worry. You can trust Me"? I don't think I can handle that response from Him in this moment. Trusting my worries to God is easier said than done.

What if God is so disappointed in my lack of faith in Him to help me that He gives up on me, turning away from a person who doesn't trust Him?

These painful questions swirl in my thoughts: *Will God be faithful when my faith in Him is weak? Has my lack of faith left me completely alone?* I found the answer when I turned in my Bible to Luke 22:43-44:

"Then an angel from heaven appeared and strengthened him. He prayed more fervently, and he was in such agony of spirit that his sweat fell to the ground like great drops of blood."

While Jesus prayed in the garden the night before His suffering, crucifixion and death, He asked if there could be another way, another path. Jesus prayed while in great agony, so great that His body poured out sweat like blood.

In the midst of such human anxiety, Jesus asked His Father if His circumstances could change. But God did not change His plans, even for His beloved Son. Yet, even so, God did not abandon Jesus because of His anxiety! God comforted Him, sending an angel for strength.

When "what ifs" fill my mind and magnify the uncertainty of my faith in God, the truth of who God truly is and how He will respond in these moments remains. As I pray, I need to remember that God promised to do the same for us as He did for His Son. When I cry out to Him, confused and uncertain about what may lie ahead, He promised not to leave me. He will sit with me to strengthen me in love and empathy as He did with His Son.

While I still struggle with the many "what if" scenarios that come in life, I take comfort in knowing that God promises to be there to listen, comfort, strengthen and love me. He loves us through our struggles and doubts. He will be there waiting patiently for my focus to turn away from the burdens I carry, to turn back to Him in faith, ready to hear Him say "trust in Me."

And I will.

God's reassurance for me is ...

GROUNDED

TRISTA PARK

"Blessed is the man who trusts in the LORD, And whose hope is the LORD.
For he shall be like a tree planted by the waters, Which spreads out its roots by the river,
And will not fear when heat comes; But its leaf will be green, And will not be anxious
in the year of drought, Nor will cease from yielding fruit."
Jeremiah 17:7-8 (NKJV)

The months leading up to the birth of my third daughter had been a roller coaster of emotions. Halfway along in the pregnancy, a serious heart defect inevitably requiring major open-heart surgery was discovered by the doctor.

Facing the fear of the unknown, I found myself at a crossroads. I had to make a choice if I would trust God to bring me through one of the darkest seasons I had yet faced or if I would give in to the fear of unfamiliar territory.

I had faced some difficult circumstances in my lifetime, but not to this extreme. Worried I would lose my daughter at any moment felt like a heavy burden to bear and became a momentous, faith-defining journey for me.

My tiny little redhead came ready to fight as she rapidly entered this world two weeks before her due date. It was apparent from her oxygen-depleted blue skin God had not chosen to miraculously heal her heart as I had desperately prayed for weeks on end. In fact, she had a second heart defect requiring more emergent surgery.

My postpartum body felt empty, my emotions raw and heavy when the anesthesiologist came to take my two-week-old back to the operating room.

Her recovery did not go as planned, and I once again lay in the dark of night, tears streaming down my cheeks, pouring onto my pillow, my soul crying out to God to spare her life.

As her heart worked tirelessly to keep her alive, my heart was struggling to trust God through circumstances far beyond my control. If ever there was a time to put my faith into practice, it was now. Relying on what seemed like elementary verses such as, *"Trust in the LORD with all your heart"* — the very substance my faith had been founded on years ago — gave me practical help (Proverbs 3:5).

These are the faith-defining moments in our lives. The moments where we make the choice to either actively trust that God will carry us through, knowing He is our rock and refuge, or slip away into fear.

Relying on the scriptures I had memorized years before became God's grace to bring me through the two-month hospital stay, the balm my aching soul so desperately needed.

The importance of being rooted in God's Word is evident in these trials and tribulations, just as Jeremiah 17:7-8 shares: *"Blessed is the man who trusts in the LORD, And whose hope is the LORD. For he shall be like a tree planted by the waters, Which spreads out its roots by the river, And will not fear when heat comes; But its leaf will be green, And will not be anxious in the year of drought, Nor will cease from yielding fruit"* (NKJV).

The Scripture we have hidden in our hearts becomes the anchor for our weary souls, reminding us where to place our hope. There is no reason to fear when trials come because we are grounded in Him!

Friends, God may not change the circumstances you are facing. The blessing comes from our security in Christ, our salvation and our confidence in Him! God will redeem all things with His Second Coming. In the meantime, we must rest in His grace and trust in His power. We must search His Word that quenches our thirst, pray through the affliction, and know without a doubt that the greatest blessing rests in our eternal inheritance.

God's reassurance for me is ...

WHEN THE UNKNOWN HAS YOU DOUBTING

JULIE SUNNE

"But I have trusted in your faithful love; my heart will rejoice in your deliverance."
Psalm 13:5 (CSB)

The knot in my stomach tightened. Soon, I'd need to tell him. I glanced at the clock for what seemed to be the hundredth time. Any minute my boss would call it a day, and the opportunity to tell him I quit would have to wait. Yet doubt crept in. Maybe I'm being hasty. Or lazy. Or worse, foolish. Maybe there's still a way to make it work.

Quitting my part-time job at the funeral home required days of prayer and discussion with my husband. We wrestled with the implications, weighing the pros and cons. And we felt at peace about my decision to quit. As caregiver to our 21-year-old daughter with intellectual disabilities, I needed to be more available to her. So why was I hesitant to follow through? Didn't I trust God to see us through whatever consequences the change would bring?

Finally, I spun my chair to face my boss and blurted, "I have to quit!" While explaining my reasons to a somewhat surprised yet understanding man, my phone rang. It was my youngest son — he never called. I swiped up on my cell phone screen. "Hi hon, what's up?"

Any previous doubt about quitting quickly melted away as Joey explained that once again, no one had shown up to care for Rachel. I thank God he was home on Christmas break and would watch his sister until my husband or I made it home. Tears slipped down my cheeks. God had graciously given me the confirmation I so desired.

But why can't I trust Him without such obvious affirmation? Why do I insist on evidence of His consistent care and presence? I want to trust God no matter how uncertain or dire a situation appears. And then I read Psalm 13 and received fresh insight into how to have such faith. Our key verse, Psalm 13:5, reads, *"But I have trusted in your faithful love; my heart will rejoice in your deliverance."* Amazingly, King David penned this declaration of faith only a few verses after expressing his hopelessness in his current situation: *"How long, LORD? Will you forget me forever? How long will you hide your face from me?"* (Psalm 13:1, CSB).

From an expression of despair to a declaration of absolute certainty in his deliverance! How could King David be so certain of God's deliverance in the face of such difficult situations? The first half of verse 5 tells us: "But I have trusted in your faithful love ..." (Psalm 13:5). David had seen God's faithful love in action. God had been trustworthy in the past, and David remembered. And since God's character never changes, the king knew he could still trust Him.

We can have the faith of King David. We can trust God when all seems hopeless or uncertain. It involves reflecting and remembering. Looking back on our lives and seeing God at work. Looking back and remembering His faithful love. And as we do, we can walk confidently into an uncertain future, trusting in our unchanging, steadfast Lord.

God's reassurance for me is ...

TRUSTING GOD DURING DISAPPOINTMENT

LAURA FARHY

"Leave us alone! Let us be slaves to the Egyptians. It's better to be a slave
in Egypt than a corpse in the wilderness!"
Exodus 14:12b (NLT)

Ping! The long-awaited reply from a very important person — providing a very important opportunity that will finally materialize all my hopes and dreams in the breadth of an email — slides into my inbox. I did it. This is happening! My heart surges with glee. I knew God was going to open this door. I believed He would, and faith is like hot sauce — a little bit goes a long way.

"Thank you for your email, but we will not be moving forward on your project."

Wait, what? No. This is a mistake. Believe and receive. I believed, so why am I not receiving? God, I followed You into the desert. Why did You lead me here to die?

In Exodus 14, the Israelites have left Egypt and slavery behind, following Moses and God into the wilderness. But when the Egyptians pursue them, and it seems like God has left them to die, they cry out: *"Leave us alone! Let us be slaves to the Egyptians. It's better to be a slave in Egypt than a corpse in the wilderness!"* (Exodus 14:12b).

Like the Israelites, it's easy to forget all the incredible things God has done in our past when His performance is no longer predictable. Like the Israelites, out of anger or fear, we might start looking for a new Moses to tell us what we want to hear, a new god to give us what we want, and a short cut to where we want to go. But getting to the Promised Land is less about the arriving and more about the arriver.

In the wilderness on the way to the Promised Land, God used disappointment to purge what was in the hearts of the people. He unpacked all unnecessary emotional baggage from the caravan in their chests, because like an experienced pilot, He knew the precise computations required to land safely at the desired destination.

God knew if the Israelites took what was in their hearts to their Promised Land, they would inevitably destroy it before they could enjoy it. Arriving requires a prepared sojourner who can utilize the land of milk and honey judiciously.

Looking back now, I realize God didn't use my rejection to reject me. He used my rejection to reject the ailments in my heart. I know now that if I got that opportunity, I would have turned it into an idol, and my success would have been a link in the chain of a false identity that I inherited from the many pharaohs in my life. I thought my opportunity WAS my Promised Land and my emailer the gatekeeper. But only God can provide the promise of a land that satisfies our hearts' desires.

My dear sister, if you are in the wilderness and utterly disappointed because you aren't yet in the Promised Land, be encouraged. The wilderness is where God prepares you for the Promised Land. And the wilderness is where God prepares the Promised Land for you.

He can turn bread into stones, water into wine and walls into doors that no man can close. Don't look back. Keep pushing forward into a place prepared, or being prepared, just for you. Don't settle for anything less, because the best is what God intends to give you. Trust your Tour Guide's pace; He did not bring you to the wilderness to leave you but to love you.

God's reassurance for me is ...

THORNS OF GRACE

JANAE HOFER

"Therefore, in order to keep me from becoming conceited, I was given a thorn in my flesh, a messenger of Satan, to torment me. Three times I pleaded with the Lord to take it away from me. But he said to me, 'My grace is sufficient for you, for my power is made perfect in weakness.'"
2 Corinthians 12:7b-9a (NIV)

Three times? Anxiety and worry have likely led us to plead with God to take away thorns in our flesh far more than three times.

My thorn is physical: Lack of oxygen for 21 minutes following my birth resulted in my neurological disability of cerebral palsy (CP). My CP is so severe that I am unable to care for myself, talk clearly or even type more than seven words per minute unless I dictate to a typist.

One time of intense pleading occurred a few months before I began law school. I fasted and prayed for God to at least heal my speech. How could I be an attorney with unclear speech?

God did not take away my thorn. My speech and other motor skills remain afflicted even as I am presently a corporate litigation attorney.

Paul writes about his thorn in 2 Corinthians 12:7b-9a: *"Therefore, in order to keep me from becoming conceited, I was given a thorn in my flesh, a messenger of Satan, to torment me. Three times I pleaded with the Lord to take it away from me. But he said to me, 'My grace is sufficient for you, for my power is made perfect in weakness.'"*

Based on Paul's use of a scribe and the large signature ending his Galatians letter, some commentators hypothesize that his thorn was poor eyesight. (Galatians 6:11) Regardless of the exact nature of Paul's thorn, we all can relate. Thorns are not strictly physical but include any *"weaknesses," "insults," "hardships," "persecutions" or "difficulties"* (2 Corinthians 12:10).

What is your thorn? If God will not take away every thorn, how can we replace our anxiety and worry over thorns with the trust and assurance seen in Paul? We must adopt his perspective on thorns:

THORNS PREVENT CONCEITEDNESS.

Paul acknowledges that the thorn in his flesh has a purpose. The thorn keeps him *"from becoming conceited"* (v. 7). Thus, we can replace frustrations of "If only I didn't have [insert thorn], I could [insert thorn-hindered act]" with gratitude for thorn-cultivated humility and reliance upon God. For example, although I may feel I could be a more efficient and affluent attorney "If only I didn't have CP," my CP forces humble reliance upon God in my career.

THORNS POINT TO GOD'S GRACE.

Next, stripped of conceit that hinders genuine reliance, Paul pleads for relief and receives God's response. (vv. 8-9) Paul accepts God's promise of grace sufficient for him. (v. 9) If God's grace was sufficient for the Apostle Paul, His grace is certainly sufficient for us. When we plead with God, and we are open to His response, we position ourselves to identify and experience His grace anew.

THORNS SHOW GOD'S POWER.

Finally, Paul used his weaknesses to boast in Christ's power. We can follow suit — allowing a display of Christ's power in our accomplishments in light of our thorns. God loves showcasing His power through weakness. Look at Moses (Exodus 3-4) and David. (1 Samuel 16:1-13)

We can delight in our thorns upon seeing the resulting humility, sufficing grace and anointing power that comes through thorns. May we replace our anxiety over life's thorns with delight in experiencing God's grace and showing His power as we humbly rely on Him.

God's reassurance for me is ...

HOW DOES YOUR EMOTIONAL GARDEN GROW?

KELLY SMITH

"May the God of hope fill you with all joy and peace as you trust in him,
so that you may overflow with hope by the power of the Holy Spirit."
Romans 15:13 (NIV)

I come from a long line of green thumbs. Granddaddy always planted more than he needed as if growing vegetables in the backyard was every American's civic duty. My grandmother, now in her mid-80s, still plants a garden each spring. My childhood summer memories include warm tomatoes and speckled strawberries from my parents' garden. My "garden" is quite the downsize — a few tomato plants in backyard containers.

Be it acres of corn or a small container garden, growing fruits and veggies is a joint effort between the gardener and the Creator. One plants and the other grows. The farmer (or novice city gardener like me) works the soil while God provides sun and rain. Growth doesn't happen without effort from both participants.

This principle helps me find my footing when my emotions overwhelm me.

I have a few tactics I use to regulate all of those big feelings on my own:
- I replace my worry with rational thoughts on the pages of my journal.
- My remedy for stress is a color-coded to-do list that mimics control.
- When my heart is wounded, I force a smile when I don't feel like it.

I try to "fix myself." My efforts are like planting a garden in a dark basement. I can dig, plant and fertilize, but nothing will grow without God's gifts of sun and rain.

When I'm out of self-help tricks, I resort to prayer. I beg God to take my hurt feelings away, give me a loving heart, or make me nice to the people that hurt me. These are all things God is very capable of doing. However, asking for a miraculous emotional overhaul is akin to expecting zucchini plants to sprout where no seeds are planted.

In Romans 15:13, Paul says, *"May the God of hope fill you with all joy and peace as you trust in him, so that you may overflow with hope by the power of the Holy Spirit"* (NIV). Paul establishes a relationship between my trust in God and God's work in me. Like the gardener and the Creator, I plant seeds of trust in God, and God produces hope, joy and peace in me.

As I release the responsibility to "fix myself," the knots in my shoulders begin to loosen. The weight of taming my emotions and healing my hurts is not mine to bear alone.

What is my responsibility in my "emotional" garden? God asks me to plant seeds of trust. Seeds of trust include remembering His faithfulness in past struggles, reminding myself of His power by reading Scripture and prayer. When I feel uncertain, hurt or stressed, my efforts are best spent trusting that God has the supernatural ability to turn my chaos into something beautiful.

When emotions overwhelm you, stop to consider how your emotional garden grows. Release the responsibility to fix your own heart. You can't force hope or strategize joy. Plant seeds of trust in God and watch Him grow an abundant crop of hope, joy and peace in you.

God's reassurance for me is ...

GOD IS

OUR HOPE AND

OUR HEALER

WHY PLAY IT SAFE?

LYNDE SWANNER

"I have told you these things, so that in me you may have peace.
In this world you will have trouble. But take heart! I have overcome the world."
John 16:33 (NIV)

Worry plagues a lot of what I do ... or don't do. I don't know about you, but I can find myself tangled in anxiety about the smallest, everyday things. This means at times I can be scared to move forward, jump, take the step, or do the hard thing because of what might happen — what hurt, injury or failure it might cause. I assume that if I live life this way, it is keeping me safe, making me immune from trouble.

However, I found out last year that you can do nothing wrong, nothing unsafe, nothing risky and still get hurt, still be sad and still end up in surgery. Calamity will visit us; it happens in this imperfect world, no matter how hard we try to keep it at bay.

Several months ago, I found myself standing in my bathroom when I noticed an odd-shaped flash of light in my eye. A gut feeling and a nudge to not ignore it led me to call the eye doctor. After an exam, they told me I had a retinal detachment. They were a *little* shocked. I was a lot shocked.

The same type of question was asked repeatedly: "Did you have an injury to the eye?"
I didn't. My behaviors and routines hadn't changed. I hadn't been hurt, hadn't tried anything risky. It just happened, unexpectedly.

I went through eye surgery, and after several weeks of healing, was released to begin normal, day-to-day activities. But I also experienced extreme caution and anxiety about completing normal, day-to-day life. I worried about bending over, lifting even very light objects — everything.

Which led to me standing on a treadmill, months after surgery, terrified to run again ... completely convinced my surgery wouldn't hold and I would lose my eyesight. All those questions came flooding back, and I realized I had done nothing to cause my injury, yet it still happened. I wanted to protect myself, but how do you prevent something from happening that didn't have a cause? It made no sense.

The words in the book of John came to me, *"In this world you will have trouble. But take heart! I have overcome the world"* (John 16:33b).

So, I ran. I lived. It was scary, but I did it.

If we can't guarantee living out of harm's way, then why do we hold back? Why do we build the walls and bubbles? Why do we play it "safe"? Why not take the steps and the risks He offers when He promises He has already been there?

Simply following Christ is a huge risk. The life He asks is a hard one. It goes against any common-sense worldview. Sometimes following Jesus means we give up the things we think steady us, the things we think give us assurance and protections.

This life is messy. There are unexpected *asks* and even more unexpected answers. If Christ-followers are living scared and timid, are we really following Christ? I asked myself these questions: *Am I really going where He asks, loving the way He loves, living crazy-faithful? Is my heart willing to make the moves or changes if He asks?*

It's about a heart willing and obedient to where He wants to take it. Safe or not.
It won't be easy; there will be bumps and bruises. Regular life can bring pain too, but with God, these bumps and bruises have a purpose, a story. Pain with God will never end you, will never be without rescue, will never come without healing.

Don't trust the world to be your safety net. Don't trust the strength of walls you've built. Let Jesus be your safety, your wings, your parachute. Because in this world, even when you're as safe as possible, trouble will visit, but we don't have to be worried and live scared, because Jesus has overcome it all.

God's reassurance for me is ...

WHEN YOU'RE DONE, GOD HAS JUST BEGUN

CHRISTINE VIRGIN

"He said: 'Listen, King Jehoshaphat and all who live in Judah and Jerusalem!
This is what the LORD says to you: "Do not be afraid or discouraged because of this vast army.
For the battle is not yours, but God's."'"
2 Chronicles 20:15 (NIV)

As we somberly got in the car after another unproductive therapy session, my husband's tired, sad words made even the hairs on my face stand up: "I'm done."

As he packed a bag to go anywhere but home, hopelessness enveloped us. We had been perplexed by our perspectives and struck down by our put-downs. Circumstances had strained us and stressed us. I cried in the shower every day because it was the only place the kids wouldn't see, and despite wanting to bury myself in a tub of ice cream, I couldn't even eat from the anxiety.

Oh, the unfairness of that!

When the odds are so stacked against us that we see no way out except the way we never wanted, despair is overwhelming. And yet, for those in Christ, God's Word stands, (Psalm 119:89) the Holy Spirit empowers, (Zechariah 4:6) and prayer works. (James 5:16)

I think Jehoshaphat knew desperation like we felt. He was King of Judah for 25 years. Despite honoring the Lord with his reign, a vast army gathered to annihilate him, his people and their land. Jehoshaphat gathered his people and called for a fast. (Apparently, he couldn't eat while stressed, either.) And there, he cried out:

"Our God, will you not judge them? For we have no power to face this vast army that is attacking us. We do not know what to do, but our eyes are on you" (2 Chronicles 20:12, NIV).

Jehoshaphat leaned into and looked to his Lord. The Lord responded:

" ... 'Do not be afraid or discouraged because of this vast army. For the battle is not yours, but God's'" (2 Chronicles 20:15b, c).

Trusting God, they praised the Lord as they headed toward the battlefield. When they arrived, the armies that had amassed to take them out had instead annihilated each other. It took Jehoshaphat and the people of Judah three days to carry the plunder back home.

During our greatest struggles and most unfair times, when we are confused and without answers, God is there. He is nearest to us when we are brokenhearted, (Psalm 34:18) reminding us that He is fighting our battles.

For months, I read 2 Chronicles 20 almost every day, clinging to Jesus, trusting His Word and praying God would fight for us. And He did.

It's been nearly four years, and while no marriage is perfect, by the grace of God, ours is healing. God resurrects. He refurbishes, renews, remolds, repairs and raises from the dead.

I don't know how God will work in your circumstances, or whether you will experience healing on this side of eternity or in heaven. But I do know God loves to give good gifts to His children, and He rejoices in answering your prayers. Nothing is too hard for Him. For when you're done, God has just begun.

God's reassurance for me is ...

HOPE FOR WHEN YOUR LIFE FEELS LIKE A COUNTRY MUSIC SONG

MEREDITH CARR

"Though the fig tree should not blossom, nor fruit be on the vines, the produce of the olive fail and the fields yield no food, the flock be cut off from the fold and there be no herd in the stalls, yet I will rejoice in the LORD; I will take joy in the God of my salvation."
Habakkuk 3:17-18 (ESV)

Growing up in the south, I became well-acquainted with the gloomy basics of country music songs: your truck breaks down, your partner leaves you and your dog dies. I used to chuckle at this clichéd melodrama when I was a young girl and couldn't imagine life falling apart.

However, I remember waking up one day and thinking: My life has become a country music song. My marriage was a mess, my child was struggling deeply, and my own health buckled under the weight of postpartum depression and anxiety.

I felt crippled by a hopelessness that made me question if life would ever hold joy again. Would I ever wake up to a day that didn't feel crushed by stress before the sun even rose? Would the buzzing ball of anxiety tightly tucked inside my gut ever disappear?

I wonder if you have ever asked these questions. Perhaps your life feels like a bad country music song, too. Maybe your path is littered with broken relationships, broken promises, broken everything, just like mine. You look around and see only angst.

In the Old Testament book of Habakkuk, we find an ancient "country music song" of sorts that speaks into this angst of a life in distress:

"Though the fig tree should not blossom, nor fruit be on the vines, the produce of the olive fail and the fields yield no food, the flock be cut off from the fold and there be no herd in the stalls, yet I will rejoice in the LORD; I will take joy in the God of my salvation" (Habakkuk 3:17-18).

Like Habakkuk, we may look around and see only lack. Our *"fig tree"* might be a relationship or our health. Our "flock" might be our heart's deepest dreams. And yet, the ancient hope in these words still stands true for us: We can walk through the desolate valley and still find joy in our God!

The enemy wants us linking our hope and joy to what our eyes can see. He wants us chasing the phantom of a perfect life instead of chasing our perfect Father who holds every detail of our lives in His sovereign hands — even when we're trudging through the valley.

Our God graciously gives us salvation, both in heaven and here on earth. Right here in the middle of the stress and anxiety. Right here in the middle of all the things we wish were different. Right here in the scary middle of the story, where we cannot yet see the ending God is writing.

Today, let us join the faith-filled cry of Habakkuk and choose joy, despite what our human eyes see. Life might feel like a bad country music song, but God has promised He will *"rejoice over [us] with singing"* (Zephaniah 3:17, NIV).

And no matter the bleakness of our circumstances, God will never ever leave nor forsake us. He surrounds us with *"songs of deliverance"* (Psalm 32:7, NIV), weaving our pain into an exquisite chorus of redemption.

May that be the song we sing in the midst of these valley days.

God's reassurance for me is ...

WHEN "WHY" REMAINS UNANSWERED

TERESA FRITSCHLE

"I have told you these things so that in me you may have peace."
John 16:33a (CSB)

"Why?"

It's one of the first questions we ask when we begin to speak. As children, the question helps us learn about the world. It also helps us learn the difference between right and wrong. But at some point, it will be a cry born out of suffering.

The most difficult year of my life began in the summer of 2008, when my father passed away unexpectedly at the age of 65. We were celebrating his retirement and looking forward to the adventures ahead of him and my mom. They had so many plans. And just like that, it was over. Why?

A brief eight months later, I was diagnosed with breast cancer at the age of 41. Again, why?

During that year of loss and sickness, I wrestled with God a lot. I literally screamed the question into heaven. "WHY, LORD?"

Here's the thing — my head knows this is a fallen world. The sin born in the Garden of Eden brought death and sickness with it. On top of that, as much as I wish it weren't true, I'm not perfect. We all mess up a lot. And Jesus tells us in John 16:33 we will experience suffering. There I was in the thick of it. And I thought if I only knew why, I would feel so much better. If I knew why, it would all make sense, and I would have some peace.

But there weren't any answers to my whys. Nobody could tell me why God had called my dad home when He did. And not even science could tell me why I had cancer, with no family history or genetic markers present.

Then one night, as I was crying out to the Lord, 1 Corinthians 13:12 whispered in response. God reminded me that sometimes it's enough if He knows why: *"For now we see only a reflection as in a mirror, but then face to face. Now I know in part, but then I will know fully, as I am fully known"* (CSB).

This took me back to John 16:33: *"I have told you these things so that in me you may have peace. You will have suffering in this world. Be courageous! I have conquered the world."*

Jesus tells us we will experience suffering. But first, He promises us peace in Him. As I realized God was asking me to hand my whys over to Him, to trust Him with them, I found the bridge between my suffering and Christ's promised peace.

God is trustworthy and faithful in all things. I know everything I need to know right now, because I know Him. If He wants or needs me to know more, I will. But when there is no answer to why, I need to stop and ask "who?" instead. That question always has an answer: God. And He is good.

God's reassurance for me is ...

GROWING INSIDE AND UNDERNEATH

DESIREE MCCULLOUGH

"That according to the riches of his glory he may grant you to be strengthened with power through his Spirit in your inner being, so that Christ may dwell in your hearts through faith — that you, being rooted and grounded in love, may have strength to comprehend with all the saints what is the breadth and length and height and depth, and to know the love of Christ that surpasses knowledge, that you may be filled with all the fullness of God."
Ephesians 3:16-19 (ESV)

The bark was weathered, cracked and a shade somewhere between gray and misery. Its bare branches formed sharp points that screamed toward heaven. Its two-trunk deviation revealed a war within itself.

My husband figured our new home came with a dead walnut tree, but I was more hopeful. As fall and winter days grew harsher and shorter, I stared out my kitchen window at our timeworn tree. Tribes of magpies decided it was their designated spot for screeching out concerns. Whipping winds threatened to snap branches. Snow weighed heavily on its weak frame.

I became drawn to this tangle of exhausted creation because I knew this tree. I was this tree.

No one is exempt from the harshness of life, but I've let it wear me down to bare boughs many times. Thirteen moves in 14 years. Financial seasons that made me want to fold my college diploma into a paper airplane. Worrying about the future of both a parent and a child. Then, there's the fight to look "normal," "together" and "under control" to the world.

But a voice calls loudly in these seasons.

Inside and underneath, child.

God calls us to let Him build up what is not visible to the outside world even though we're eager to show we're okay on the surface. Through Paul, we see the need to ask for spiritual strength inside and underneath:

"That according to the riches of his glory he may grant you to be strengthened with power through his Spirit in your inner being, so that Christ may dwell in your hearts through faith — that you, being rooted and grounded in love, may have strength to comprehend with all the saints what is the breadth and length and height and depth, and to know the love of Christ that surpasses knowledge, that you may be filled with all the fullness of God" (Ephesians 3:16-19).

Paul echoes these points to two other churches. As the stresses and afflictions of this world tear us down, we can be confident knowing our inner self is in constant renewal. (2 Corinthians 4:16) Walking in faith with our Savior means we are to root and ground ourselves in Him. (Colossians 2:6-7) Firmly established in our God, let Him fill you even when branches are breaking and leaves are falling.

When we "just don't feel like it" or have nothing left, grow where they can't see, friend. Inside and underneath, child.

Spring came around. My husband was hidden somewhere high in our tree, cutting bountiful, fragrant branches that overtook the roof of our shed. Stunned, I hardly noticed it was changing in magnificent yet subtle ways. "Lord," I smiled, "You always knew. You always saw."

May our inner being be strengthened with the Lord's power when we experience our deepest "winters." We may be stuck in the midst of chaos, but may the Spirit root and ground us deeply in the foundation of His love in constant fellowship with Him.

God's reassurance for me is ...

GOD IS
_____

FAITHFUL
_____

AND ALWAYS
_____

ON TIME
_____

BETWEEN THE LIFE YOU HAD AND THE ONE YOU WANT

JADA MCCLINTICK

"Wait for the LORD; be strong, and let your heart take courage; wait for the LORD!"
Psalm 27:14 (ESV)

It's not that I don't trust God to answer my prayers — it's that I don't trust how long He takes.

I was lonely after my divorce. Time had passed and healed my wounds. I spent time with friends, went to movies, threw myself into activities, work and hanging out with my kids. But sometimes I just wanted a partner to go to dinner with. Someone to hold my hand, take a walk and talk to about the details of my day. On some days I was fulfilled. But other days all I could think was, single stinks.

The Lord knew my heart and we had talked often about my longing for companionship. So, I decided to be direct in my prayers and ask Him to bring me a husband. After delivering my prayerful request to the Lord, I waited … and waited … and waited. Then my waiting turned to worry.

Did the Lord hear me?
Does He even care?
What is taking so long?

Oftentimes, we trust God with everything but His timetable. If He doesn't do something at the exact moment we think He should, we wonder if He ever will.

If we aren't careful, our worry about how long the Lord is taking can turn into outright anxiety. It feels as though there is a looming gap between our old circumstance and the one we hope for. In the gap, fear and uncertainty are born.

In between the life where I was a wife and my prayer to be married again was a fearful gap. I was living in the middle of a prayer and provision, a worried, fearful cavern echoing with the chorus … *will I always be alone?*

Often when the waiting feels hard, we try to fill the gap with our own plans. We manipulate the gap. It can seem as though God isn't working fast enough or isn't moving at all!

But here is a secret: Something else lives in the middle of the gap.

In our key verse, King David gives us a clue: *"Wait for the LORD; be strong, and let your heart take courage; wait for the LORD!"* (Psalm 27:14)

In the gap between the prayer and the provision is trust. You can trust the Lord because He loves you and will never disappoint you. Don't give up!

You know what else "gap" is in the middle of? "Gap" also sits in the middle of "agape."

Agape is the type of love that defines who God is. The God we can trust to come through in the fearful and unknown in-between places. Eventually God did deliver my husband — in His perfect timing. We have no reason to be fearful or anxious in our waiting. All we really need to be doing in the gap is trusting God and His agape love for us.

God's reassurance for me is ...

COLLECTING WOUNDS

MELANIE DAVIS PORTER

"Those who are dominated by the sinful nature think about sinful things, but those who are controlled by the Holy Spirit think about things that please the Spirit."
Romans 8:5 (NLT)

The waves rhythmically lapped the shoreline as I walked on the wet sand giving way beneath my feet. I always saved my long walk for the last day of vacation. Looking for sea glass, perfect shells and unusual mementos, I realized that my collection was growing, and I could afford to be a little pickier with my choices.

The two-hour stroll provided time to reflect on the healing I so desperately needed. *Grief, loss, betrayal and rejection* ... all themes in a season of letting go and moving on. I listened as God spoke directly to my heart:

"Just like these treasures from the sea, you have chosen to pick up wounds to add to the growing collection now consuming your heart, child."

I felt a quickening in my stomach. Tears slipped below my sunglasses, rolling down sun-kissed cheeks.

The pain that comes with loss makes the heart raw and weak. This state puts us in a place where we can be easily offended because we've been greatly hurt.

It doesn't take much emotion to tip the scales of a broken heart.

As the cool ocean breeze blew the sticky strands of hair caressing my face, I knew the Father was telling me it was time to stop collecting wounds.

I realized that my deep hurts had triggered a domino effect of emotional chaos that only complicated my grief.

We can choose to pick up wounds, or we can choose to let them be. Satan longs for us to be led by the wound instead of being led by the Spirit. He is a master at manipulating our emotions. He thrives on pain and uses every opportunity to ping our deepest hurts.

Unfortunately, being led by the wound opens the door to bitterness. Being led by the wound can shut down our hearts to others and ministry. But we know the love of an all-consuming God who wants us thriving in wholeness.

You see ... just because a painful moment or experience taps us on the shoulder doesn't mean we have to turn around to greet it.

When I finally cried out to God and begged Him to heal me, I immediately felt His prompting to change my thinking.

As today's Scripture reminds us: *"Those who are dominated by the sinful nature think about sinful things, but those who are controlled by the Holy Spirit think about things that please the Spirit"* (Romans 8:5).

It's so easy to let our sinful nature make us think the worst when we've been wounded, isn't it?

I found that dwelling on the hurt led to sinful attitudes and divisive thinking ... which merely opened the door to more wounds. The more we dwell on a hurt, the more we rebel.

Letting go of the past while abandoning future flawed perceptions (and direct or indirect offenses) is the only way to break free from a broken heart.

I'm so grateful the Spirit sweetly reminds me that no wound is worth the trade of emotional freedom. Just like the seaside treasures I carefully collected or left behind that day, I'm now walking past the unnecessary wounds that are meant to keep me in bondage.

God's reassurance for me is ...

WAITING ON GLORY

SUZANNE SMITH

"Did I not tell you that if you believed, you would see the glory of God?"
John 11:40 (NIV)

We knew it was coming. My husband lost his job due to the company's profit loss. Twenty-five years of loyal employment were gone in one day. What we did not expect was the 13 months of unemployment.

At first, there was excitement of new adventures and new possibilities. This could be a good thing!

However, days became months. There were interviews and even call backs, but no offers. Our money was dwindling. By Christmas, we were living off money my mother-in-law sent us. My mother had to pay for a car repair. The unemployment checks were only a few weeks from ending, and then we would file for bankruptcy. Any hope of new possibilities were gone. We were brought to our knees.

I found myself asking more questions of God rather than trusting Him. *What are You doing? Do You hear us? Are You punishing us?* I woke up every day with a free-fall sensation in my gut, and for the first time in my life, I knew what it felt like to go hungry. I felt anxious when anyone at church asked. It was a tired story with no resolve, and singing worship songs only made me question a "Good, Good Father." Quite often, my drives to work were filled with tears and prayer: "God, please help us."

My heart broke into pieces the day my husband confessed, "I don't think the prayers are working." We were waiting on the Lord, but we were feeling forgotten.

God kept bringing me back to this one question Jesus asks of Martha in the story of Lazarus in John 11:40: *"... Did I not tell you that if you believed, you would see the glory of God?"* (NIV)

I felt the same urgency and grief as Mary and Martha. Like me, they knew their friend Jesus loved Lazarus and was able to fix their situation, and so, they sent for Him. When Jesus did not show up "in time," it seemed all was lost, but death is only permanent by human standards. You see, Jesus had a divine purpose in waiting. He could have simply healed Lazarus and called it a day. Instead, He waited until Lazarus was dead long enough to make your nose hairs curl from the stench. Why? To make God known and to give life to impossibilities.

We were bankrupt and our hope was in the tomb. We needed Him to give life to what seemed impossible. After 13 months of unemployment, we had exhausted all our leads, money and intellect. Then, He opened our tomb and provided more than a salary and food on the table. He provided an opportunity for me and our daughter to attend college, tuition-free. Something we could not have done on our own with just any job. Only God can do that.

I would have preferred an easier road and plenty on the dinner table, but without the struggle, we would have missed the amazing glory of God.

God's reassurance for me is ...

BUT FIRST ... TRUST

GINA GROVE

"For this is what the LORD, the God of Israel, says: 'The jar of flour will not be used up and the jug of oil will not run dry until the day the LORD sends rain on the land.'"
1 Kings 17:14 (NIV)

I watched the deer plod slowly on its well-worn path in the snow, laser-focused on our neighbor's apple tree. A winter-dead tree, stripped of fruit for weeks now. But the deer persisted.

Boy, could I relate. For months I'd followed my own well-worn patterns. I'd stepped out of the classroom, still loving the students, but beaten down by other aspects of the job. I knew emotional healing would take time. Yet two years later, I methodically plodded along most days, pushing through old routines, expecting fresh results.

I'd completed life coach training. But with certification in hand, I had done nothing to find clients. Fear froze me. Uncertainty undid my resolve. And failure waited to welcome me home.

The widow of Zarephath knew fear and uncertainty, picking up each stick, fingers trembling, tears running down her face. Feeling the hopelessness in her routine of gathering branches, stoking a small fire, making a final loaf for her son with their bit of flour and oil ... only to eventually die of starvation after the paltry meal was consumed. (1 Kings 17:12)

But God's focus never left the widow, her son or the prophet. He told Elijah, *"I have instructed a widow there to supply you with food"* (1 Kings 17:9b, NIV). I bet that was news to the widow!

"Elijah said to [the widow], 'Don't be afraid. Go home and do as you have said. But first make a small loaf of bread for me from what you have and bring it to me, and then make something for yourself and your son. For this is what the LORD, the God of Israel, says: "The jar of flour will not be used up and the jug of oil will not run dry until the day the LORD sends rain on the land"'" (1 Kings 17:13-14).

"But first ..."

The widow had a reasonable plan. But first, God asked her to release fear and consider a different way.

But first, God offered her hope in the opportunity of serving another.
But first, He asked her to trust His providence beyond what her eyes saw in the jar and the jug.

Picking up the same sticks and kindling a fire of self-pity won't ignite hope. Routines are important, but first, ask God for eyes that look up for opportunities and forward with trust.

Sweet friend, it's time to stop nibbling in fear on our small, safe loaves. Pick up new sources of hope and strength, knowing God will supply the flour (gluten-free if necessary!) and oil we need to cook up something truly good. A God who gave His own Son to fill our deepest needs will always give us exactly what we need. But first ... take a minute to breathe in God's grace and peace, letting go of fear and moving forward in the freedom of God's bounty and love.

God's reassurance for me is ...

ARE YOU SINKING IN THE WAVES GOD CALLED YOU TO WALK ON?

KRISTIN TREZZA

"Jesus immediately reached out his hand and took hold of him, saying to him, 'O you of little faith, why did you doubt?' And when they got into the boat, the wind ceased."
Matthew 14:31-32 (ESV)

Have you ever felt like you somehow ended up in the wrong life? Like you're failing in every area possible — motherhood, marriage, work, friendships — and you're not sure how to get on track with any of it? Which leads you to wonder ... are you even on the right track?

Far more often than I would like to admit, I have argued with God that He must have picked the wrong woman. I've been absolutely certain that somewhere out there was a woman who would be more patient with my kids, more loving toward my husband, more understanding of the needs of the people in my life, more capable at doing my job ... just better at being me.

I don't believe God messes up. But when you are drowning in your own anxiety and insecurities, everything can get a bit fuzzy.

The other day, I heard someone telling the story of Peter walking on water (Matthew 14:22-33), and it hit me in a way it never has before. This time, as I listened, I was Peter. And the impossible waters, my life.

I often feel as though I am living from sinking moment to sinking moment. Never actually walking on the waters of this life I've been called to, but continuously being pulled up for air by the grace of God. I've wrestled with God, insisting that I am not equipped for this life — that someone else would be better at it and that I'm here by mistake.

I try to take control, doing everything in my power to be "better," only to wind up flailing as I attempt to break free from the waves of doubt and insecurity around me.

And every time, when I turn back to Jesus, He is there with peace and reassurance. Like He did for Peter, He takes my hand, and the waves stop.

"Jesus immediately reached out his hand and took hold of him, saying to him, 'O you of little faith, why did you doubt?' And when they got into the boat, the wind ceased" (Matthew 14:31-32).

When doubts arise, Jesus lovingly reminds me that I didn't choose myself for this life. He did. He chose me for it, and He will see me through it ... if I just keep my eyes on Him. If I just trust that He is in control, even when everything feels hopeless.

God doesn't call us to live easy lives, sitting in our proverbial boats of safety, watching life float by us. He calls us instead to rely on His strength and His power, rather than our own. Because His plans are far greater than anything we could handle alone.

Life may feel impossible sometimes. There will be moments of overwhelm, hopelessness and discouragement. The waves of fear and doubt will try their hardest to engulf us. But if we keep our focus on Jesus, the author and perfecter of our faith, He is faithful to pull us out of the waves and lead us atop the impossible waters of this life.

When we keep our focus on Him and His promises, it is there we find peace.

God's reassurance for me is ...

GOD IS
SOVEREIGN
AND BIGGER THAN
OUR PROBLEMS

SEEING OUR PROBLEMS IN PROPER PERSPECTIVE

MELISSA LABIENIEC

"For this light momentary affliction is preparing for us an eternal weight of glory beyond all comparison."
2 Corinthians 4:17 (ESV)

They were massive. Just massive. Observing whales off the coast of Cape Cod last summer, I could not get over their size. Truly breathtaking.

Earlier that week, as I packed for my whale-watching trip, I could barely muster any excitement other than the anticipation of escaping what felt like a vice for a couple of days. Barreling forward in ways I didn't want, I felt forced to pacify everyone and succumb to everything the people in my world wanted of me.

Go to this. Serve at that. Fix this problem. Feel this way. Change your mind. Do it all. Ever-snowballing, unwanted expectations were weighing me down heavily and all at once. Getting away felt like my only sane option. If I wanted to remember how to breathe, I needed a reprieve. For just a moment, I wanted to forget about what everybody else wanted, needed and expected from me.

As I looked upon these creatures from the boat, I realized something. Something obvious, yet profound to me. As big as the whales were, the sea was so much bigger. The whales were but a part of something larger, deeper, vast and infinitely more powerful: the ocean.

Viewed in the proper context of the sea, the whales that minutes before appeared huge now looked like shrimp. No matter how enormous their presence seemed for a time, they always slipped back under the giant surface of the water.

Enjoying the voyage that day, it hit me: Was I too busy looking at the "whales" in my life? Was I completely missing the ocean? Was I failing to see that my circumstances, no matter how massive to me, were little compared to God?

Second Corinthians 4:17 came to my mind: *"For this light momentary affliction is preparing for us an eternal weight of glory beyond all comparison".*

To us, turmoil seems heavy and debilitating. But in perspective to eternity with Him? Our lives and any momentary issues in them can suddenly appear smaller and less overwhelming.

Yes, we get tired, weary and confused. Our problems will never be nothing. We are human, but as long as we lay our burdens at His feet and understand the issues we face are actually part of what prepares us for the beauty and love which awaits us, we can face anything. It won't negate our hurts and frustrations, but it can help us gain a fresh outlook.

Life's troubles will not actually shrink, but realizing God is so much bigger makes them appear that much smaller. The whales and sea remind us God will always have the last say.

God's reassurance for me is ...

HOW THE DETOURS OF OUR MISTAKES LEAD TO MILESTONES OF MERCY

SANDELL SNYDER

"Have mercy on me, O God, according to your unfailing love; according to your great compassion blot out my transgressions."
Psalm 51:1 (NIV)

"Where's your water bottle?" my friend asked as we neared the bottom of the mountain. Our climb to the overlook had been exhilarating, the view photo-worthy. But in my photo-snapping eagerness, I had set down my bottle and left it behind.

Ugh! Self-criticism erupted. Frustration and regret dampened the joy of the hike.

Time was short that afternoon, and so I set out on my mistake-driven detour at dawn the next morning, retracing my steps up the mountain. I arrived at the overlook as the sun rose from behind the foothills. It was breathtaking — even better than the day before.

As I approached my wayward water bottle, glistening in glorious first light, it occurred to me: The detours of our mistakes can lead to milestones of God's mercy.

I had not planned to travel that path again. Yet our compassionate God used that detour to bless me with a glimpse of His glory and a new perspective. Mistakes were made, it's true — but mercy redeemed them in a remarkable way.

Mistakes and bad decisions regularly paralyze me. I stare, fixing my gaze on the unavoidable, far-reaching consequences. How do I move forward when my failure has irrevocably changed the course of my life? What do I do with that shame and anxiety?

I found an answer in the story of David and Bathsheba in 2 Samuel 11-12. King David made a series of increasingly bad decisions, including sleeping with another man's wife and then having that man killed to conceal it. So God sent a prophet to confront him. David's response shows us how to face failure without getting stuck:

"Have mercy on me, O God, according to your unfailing love; according to your great compassion blot out my transgressions" (Psalm 51:1).

When David found himself far from God's path, he humbly acknowledged his sin, but then he turned his attention toward who God is. Instead of becoming paralyzed in shame and seeking mercy out of fear, he trusted in God's unfailing love and compassion. That focus on God and expectation of His goodness made all the difference. He turned his face toward his King and worshipped.

As David retraced his steps back toward the Lord, he received an unexpected blessing. Solomon, the second-born son of David and Bathsheba, became a milestone of mercy on the detour of David's mistakes. God loved Solomon and He raised him up as heir to David's throne. But even more amazing — the lineage of Jesus is traced through Solomon! Not only did God have mercy on David's mistakes, but He wove the milestones of that long, hard detour into His plan of salvation for all men.

If the compassionate love of God can be revealed in the detours of water bottles and wayward kings, and the redemption of mistakes can bless generations, surely your own path will be marked by milestones of incredible mercy as you turn your gaze to your King and worship.

God's reassurance for me is ...

IT COULDN'T BE EASIER

LISA APPELO

"Which is easier, to say to the paralytic, 'Your sins are forgiven,' or to say,
'Rise, take up your bed and walk'?"
Mark 2:9 (ESV)

My van was filled with flowers from my husband's funeral.

Six days earlier, I'd gone to bed happily married and woken up a sudden widow and single mom to seven. The days since had been a blur of unthinkable decisions and gut-wrenching conversations with our children.

In what should have been a weekend to celebrate Father's Day, I looked at burial plots, wrote an obituary and made sure the kids had clothes for their dad's memorial service.

Grief was crushing. But almost as hard was my overwhelm at what lay ahead.

I was filled with fear. How in the world would God heal eight broken hearts? How was I going to raise boys to men without their dad? What about my 4- and 6-year-olds who would barely remember their dad?

I was worried about money. I was paralyzed by new tasks. And I was daunted by the staggering number of parenting, financial, household and estate decisions I was now making alone.

As I drove with funeral flowers filling the backseat and fear badgering my emotions, I recalled the story of the paralytic man whose four friends put him on a mat and took him to Jesus for healing.

Mark 2 tells us Jesus was preaching in a house so crowded, the friends couldn't get in. Undeterred, they went up on the roof, cut a hole and lowered the paralytic to the ground right in front of Jesus and the gathered crowd. Then, to the astonishment of the scribes and Pharisees in the room, Jesus told the paralytic his sins were forgiven. Blasphemy, the scribes and Pharisees thought to themselves.

Jesus, knowing their thoughts, challenged them with a question: *"Which is easier, to say to the paralytic, 'Your sins are forgiven,' or to say, 'Rise, take up your bed and walk'?"* (Mark 2:9).

Jesus had authority over both — paralysis and forgiveness of sins. He went on to heal the paralyzed man, who stood, picked up his mat and praised the Lord.

That day in the van, these verses brought needed clarity. I had trusted God to forgive my sins. Why would I worry over lesser things?

We trust God for our salvation and then worry He can't supply our needs.
We trust God for our eternal destination and then fear where He might take us next week.

The bills and estate work and decisions and raising seven kids to adulthood I feared so much? That was easy for God.

What is worrying you? What problem seems unsolvable or insurmountable? Whatever it may be, it couldn't be easier for God.

God's reassurance for me is ...

ESCAPING THE RABBIT HOLE OF WORRY

JESSICA CARR

"Can any one of you by worrying add a single hour to your life?"
Matthew 6:27 (NIV)

I was no longer approaching the rabbit hole of worry — I was sprinting down it.

My mind and body were running 100 miles per hour. I had dinner cooking on the stove, my hands buried in a sink full of dishes, and I was checking off items on my to-do list in my head.

The worries of tomorrow played through my mind while I stressed about having only 24 hours in a day to complete my ever-growing list of demands and obligations.

I was letting my mind think in multiple directions when the phrase, If you do not stop worrying, you're going to worry yourself to death, popped into my mind.

 I froze.

With a dish still in my hand, I replayed the words over and over again:

"Stop worrying."

"You're going to worry yourself to death."

I've heard the phrase a hundred times, but the weight of the words had finally hit me.

Worrying brings death.

While worrying may not bring physical death, it brings death to the here and now. It forces our minds to move to a time and place that doesn't yet exist.

We allow it to create mountains and obstacles before the day ever arrives, robbing us of our peace of mind and stealing our ability to be present in life's everyday moments.

In Matthew 6:27, Jesus asks, *"Can any one of you by worrying add a single hour to your life?"*

And even though the Scripture is presented as a question, we all know the answer is: No.

But how do we stop worrying?

Philippians 4:6-7 reminds us, *"Do not be anxious about anything, but in every situation, by prayer and petition, with thanksgiving, present your requests to God. And the peace of God, which transcends all understanding, will guard your hearts and your minds in Christ Jesus"* (NIV).

So, I began to thank God for providing for the now and cast off my worries for tomorrow. I asked Him to guard my heart and mind from the worries of my to-do list and the amount of time I had to complete it.

And in that moment, I was finally able to stop sprinting down the rabbit hole of worry and see the light that has always been there, waiting to guide me back to the here and now, and give me a peace that transcends my understanding.

For every situation, big or small, we are able to turn our worries over to God. He longs to hear from us, and He will provide peace that only He can give. He is able to guard our hearts and minds from worry.

Knowing God provides peace from everyday hardships, take comfort in humbly presenting your worries before Him.

God's reassurance for me is ...

DROWNING IN MEASURED DUST

MEAGAN SUNDUST

"Who has measured the waters in the hollow of his hand and marked off the heavens with a span, enclosed the dust of the earth in a measure and weighed the mountains in scales and the hills in a balance?"
Isaiah 40:12 (ESV)

Here in the southern Arizona desert, we have beautiful and vibrant sunsets — hot pink, bright orange and deep purple fill the sky. I don't know all the scientific details behind them, but from what I understand, the lack of moisture and all the dust particles in the air allow the setting sun's light to shine through more vibrantly and colorfully than in other regions. It's beautiful dust!

Not so beautiful are our dust storms, or haboobs, as they are called, in the summer monsoon season. Haboobs are like white-outs, but instead of snow, you can't see through the dust. From miles distant, you watch a giant wall of dust march against the city and besiege it. But if you're unfortunate enough to be outside in the middle of one, you get bombarded. Dust in and on your eyes, hair, skin, clothes, mouth, ears and nose.

Sometimes life feels like that! My children are sick again. I can't keep up at work. My car is making a noise that, though I'm no mechanic, I'm pretty sure cars aren't supposed to make. My heart is still cracked and chipped from heartbreak and divorce. My friend is in the hospital. Bills are due. I see stories on the news of tragedy and suffering. God, I'm drowning in dust! Do You notice?

But the Bible tells us that God has *"enclosed the dust of the earth in a measure"* (Isaiah 40:12b). He knows exactly how many dust particles are in each engulfing haboob, and He knows every single detail of our lives. Our dust is measured out by His loving hand.

Ecclesiastes 3:11 reveals to us that God *"... has made everything beautiful in its time."* Just as God uses the dust to paint a beautiful sunset in the Arizona sky, He will use the difficult circumstances in my life to make something beautiful. Though I wish I could already see the end result, I can't know God's plan from beginning to end or how He will make something beautiful from all of the hardships in my life, but I can choose to trust that He will use them.

The Apostle Paul wrote, *"... He who began a good work in you will bring it to completion at the day of Jesus Christ"* (Philippians 1:6, ESV). This tells us that even when the haboobs of life seem to swallow us up, God is still at work. He is still the God who holds the dust of the earth in a scale! So, let's wipe off our eyes, take one step at a time through the dust, and look forward to the glorious sunset He's creating.

God's reassurance for me is ...

RESCUED FROM THE UH-OH PLACE

ASHLEY BOSWELL

"Then call on me when you are in trouble, and I will rescue you, and you will give me glory."
Psalm 50:15 (NLT)

The winter weather was unpredictable. One day I was bundled in long-sleeve layers, and the next day, the sun was warming my exposed arms. The horses in our equine-assisted therapy program boasted thick winter coats. They were confused by the sun's new warmth.

A drastic change in temperature is not optimal for horses and can cause physical stress. As I scanned the pasture, I noticed our red-coated horse, Jack. He was curling his upper lip as if to demonstrate his disapproval of this change in temperature. Jack was rescued several years earlier from a neglectful environment and now served as a "horse counselor" for people suffering from trauma.

I watched closely as Jack meandered away from the herd and plopped to the ground, creating a dust cloud as he landed. He curled his upper lip again and let out a deep groan. My heart sank. This was not the first time this week he behaved oddly. It was clear — Jack was not well.

He was drinking, eating and digesting properly. His temperature and heart rate were normal, so what could be wrong?

I left a message for the vet and waited. Searching my mind and Google for an answer just produced more panic. I felt helpless and overwhelmed, unable to provide relief for our precious Jack.

Helpless and overwhelmed. Have you been there? It's the place when we realize we are not in control and don't have all the answers. I like to call it the UH-OH place, where we Underestimate Him (UH), and as a result, feel Overwhelmed and Helpless (OH).

When we finally arrive here, we are weary, worried and asking why. If only we would cry out to Him, *"Arise, LORD! Lift up your hand, O God. Do not forget the helpless"* (Psalm 10:12, NIV).

Desperately wanting to heal Jack's pain, I stretched my arms across his broad belly and asked the Lord to give me insight into the source of his distress. Instantly, I recalled an email from a friend I received a week prior saying she was praying for our ministry and the health of our horses. She specifically mentioned she felt led to pray that our horses would be protected from colic.

Colic in horses describes the symptoms of abdominal pain that can be caused by environmental factors, including drastic changes in weather. Jack was clearly demonstrating signs of colic! The Almighty had prepared for the battle against Jack's abdominal pain even before it existed. Arrows of healing prayers were already in motion.

We aren't promised a problem-free life, but we do not have to live in an UH-OH place. Psalm 50:15 says, *"Then call on me when you are in trouble, and I will rescue you, and you will give me glory."* When we cry out to Him and trust His sovereign ability to provide for us, our feelings of helplessness and overwhelm evaporate.

Let's bring Him glory today as we overcome overwhelm by refusing to underestimate His sovereignty.

God's reassurance for me is ...

WHEN THE WEIGHT OF ANXIETY WON'T LIFT

SARAH BETH MARR

"The heavens declare the glory of God, and the sky above proclaims his handiwork."
Psalm 19:1 (ESV)

The air was beginning to turn brisk, leaves hinting of orange, yellow and red. I drove my routine route to the carpool line. My shoulders throbbed from the tension of toting anxiety around like a weighty blanket. It had been a distressing season, perhaps the most exhausting of my life. I couldn't seem to unburden my heart from anxiety and worry over one of my children.

Doctor's visits, unanswered questions, Googling for answers, whispering prayers for guidance, and wondering if we would find the help we needed preoccupied my mind most days. Every car ride where I was solo for a few minutes became a desperate prayer for God's help and healing.

I reached a standstill at the stoplight to prepare to turn right. A cluster of blackbirds caught my eye as they danced in unison — right, left, up and down. As if they had rehearsed this dance oodles of times, they lined themselves up perfectly side by side and in one swift, fluid swoosh descended from the air and onto the power line. I glanced up in awe as they perched on the power line side by side, a line of 20 or so of them, catching a breath before their next choreographed flight.

A flicker of hope stirred in my heart as I turned right and remembered Psalm 19:1: *"The heavens declare the glory of God, and the sky above proclaims his handiwork."* If the God of the universe can create the birds to glide through the air in a choreographed dance, I can trust that the God of the universe is choreographing a dance with my life.

I pulled into the junior high parking lot a little bit lighter in my heart. My problems were not untangled. I still had pending questions. I still wondered how God would come through. But the tension of my anxiety broke for the afternoon as I pondered the Master Choreographer's handiwork in creation and handiwork in my own life.

Perhaps you are under anxiety's weight today too. Maybe you're praying for answers, but the answers don't seem to be coming. Maybe you're feeling hopeless for help and desperate for the anxiety and stress to lift. You've tried to shake the tension off by simply blocking the anxiety out of your mind, or you've tried searching the internet for answers. Maybe you've run out of prayers to pray, or you've lost hope for a breakthrough.

When the weight of anxiety won't lift, let the One who choreographed creation into place lift your head. Look up and out and all around you and consider the artistry of God's creation. Notice the intricate handiwork of your Creator and allow the wonder of His care in creation to settle your anxiety.

God is choreographing a miraculous dance with your life, and you can trust Him to orchestrate every detail. You can let go of striving to figure out your next step and trust the One who wants to lead your life. Your heart can be free from the burden of anxiety as you trust God with the dance of your life.

God's reassurance for me is ...

A WAY OUT OF WORRY

SHELBY TURNER

"Search me, God, and know my heart; test me and know my anxious thoughts. See if there is any offensive way in me, and lead me in the way everlasting."
Psalm 139:23-24 (NIV)

If I could invite you into my home, you'd first see several pairs of little shoes strewn in the entryway and then a pile of toys scattered in the living room. I'd tell you not to mind the "artwork" my children recently added to the walls and I'd invite you into the kitchen so we could enjoy a cup of coffee together. In the center of my kitchen, you'd notice a big, white farmhouse kitchen sink.

I dreamed of that Joanna Gaines-inspired sink for years before we finally had the chance to redo the kitchen in our fixer-upper. The day it was installed, oh how it sparkled! I could hardly believe such a lovely scene had come to life in my very own home.

However, after only a few weeks, I found my beloved sink began to lose its sparkle. It turns out farmhouse sinks fill with dishes just like any other sink. I began to notice that with each barely nibbled dinner plate and half-drank cup of coffee plopped into the sink, its creamy white color was turning more and more yellow.

Each time I washed the dishes, I noticed the stains grew. And no matter how hard I scrubbed, the blemishes remained. I began to see the downward spiral of my sink as a picture of my life. There have been many times when I've felt like everything was aligning for me to finally have a picturesque future. It never lasts long, though, as each day seems to pile new challenges and problems on me. I end up with unsightly smudges and splotches all over what was supposed to be imperfection-free.

And this place — where what I hoped for meets what is actually true — this is the place I get stuck most deeply in heart-wrenching worry. My fears control my thoughts about today and my hopes for tomorrow. In times like these, I've learned to lean on Psalm 139:23-24:

"Search me, God, and know my heart; test me and know my anxious thoughts. See if there is any offensive way in me, and lead me in the way everlasting."

Like the imperfections that built up over time in my seemingly perfect sink, when nothing seems to be working to calm the worries the ups and downs of life bring, I know I need more than just elbow grease. I need to open my heart to the gaze of God.

I must invite God into every grimy corner and crusty crevice of my thoughts. And what will God do? He will gently and over time lead me from the dark and winding path of anxiousness to the everlasting way. And God's everlasting way is paved with fresh hope, renewed strength and His comforting presence.

If your concerns are consuming you today, ask God to search your heart. Then follow His lead when He takes your thoughts from fear to faith. He will lead you in the way out of worry!

God's reassurance for me is ...

RELEASING THE ANXIETY OF CHANGE

JULIE WIESEN

"See, I am doing a new thing! Now it springs up; do you not perceive it?
I am making a way in the wilderness and streams in the wasteland."
Isaiah 43:19 (NIV)

I'll never forget crying my way through the third grade. My family had moved, and going to a new school brought out an enormous amount of anxiety in me.

I would get to school, ask for permission to go to the bathroom, meticulously line toilet paper on the toilet seat, sit down with my clothes on and cry. I would only get up and join the class when my teacher came into the bathroom looking for me.

That's the first time I vividly remember feeling anxiety over a big life change. And it was a trend that continued for the next 30 years, whether it was bringing home a newborn from the hospital or discussing the possibility of moving across the country for my husband's job.

Change threatened me. Newness frightened me.

Change also caused some anxiety for the Israelites when they were being led out of Egypt. But the Lord encouraged them in Isaiah 43:19 when He said, *"See, I am doing a new thing! Now it springs up; do you not perceive it? I am making a way in the wilderness and streams in the wasteland."*

In the providence and sweetness of God, He led me to this verse that has been a salve to my emotions and comfort to my heart during one of the biggest changes in my life: empty nesting.

I've had to turn in the pink slip of my stay-at-home-mom job that I have occupied for 23 years.

Thankfully, there aren't any trips to the bathroom where I sit and cry all day like I did as a third-grader, no matter how tempting it has been.

Newness and change shouldn't be threatening. But, I have allowed big changes to snuff out my joy for too many years. I have let my emotions run the show, instead of letting God's truth run the show.

Even though the fact that my children no longer live at home can cause a sense of loss to fill my mind, God wants to focus my eyes on the new work He will do — just like He did with the Israelites when He told them He was doing a new thing.

In spite of being in the midst of my current circumstances, I'm excited about the path He is opening up before me because I know He will be the one leading me down it.

God's reassurance for me is ...

THE COLLISION OF GRACE

HOLLY MURRAY

"And he said unto me, My grace is sufficient for thee: for
my strength is made perfect in weakness."
2 Corinthians 12:9a (KJV)

The walls of the yellow room closed in on my 11-year-old son and I as we awaited the doctor's return. Minutes stretched into hours as we counted the holes in the tiles above his bed. I'd felt confident earlier that morning when I dropped my husband and youngest son off at church and drove to the ER. My GPS guided me, and I had trusted the doctors would promptly place a prescription in my hand for the pain in his leg. Now concern invaded my thoughts as I waited with a mask of confidence.

Just a few short days ago, my son ran in the tall summer grass with his dog at his heels.

Now as we waited together, the isolation was stifling and those joy-filled days seemed distant. Beeping sounds and the scurry of feet outside the door informed me of the untruth of my feelings, but my heart thudded harder as blood raced through my veins. Then I sensed a presence I recognized.

I heard 2 Corinthians 12:9a echo within me, *"And he said unto me, My grace is sufficient for thee: for my strength is made perfect in weakness"* (KJV). I needed grace, and the Lord had provision waiting within my reach. The lies of the enemy tried breaking through my faltering faith ... fear and what-ifs prying into my thoughts. But the sweetest, most enveloping peace pushed aside the doubts.

The doctors delivered news of a rare bone cancer, but God's grace had already collided with my circumstances and provided what we needed to withstand the diagnosis and the road ahead. In the months that followed, I watched my son encourage nurses who pricked his flesh and laugh with other children receiving chemotherapy. His hair fell out, but we grew in faith as we spoke the Word's promises for healing. Verse after verse strengthened us until God's miraculous touch disintegrated the tumor that had tried to steal our joy.

Despite difficulties of sickness, grief and financial strain, God's love provides for every need. He lavishes sufficient grace, providing strengthening joy. When our world seems to crumble, trust that His grace collides into our circumstances and His strength holds us until joy breaks through again.

God's reassurance for me is ...

GOD IS

PRESENT,

OUR PROVIDER

AND OUR

PROMISE KEEPER

RUNNING INTO THE THRONE ROOM

ELIZABETH BAKER

"Let us then approach God's throne of grace with confidence,
so that we may receive mercy and find grace to help us in our time of need."
Hebrews 4:16 (NIV)

It is hard to say which of the day's appointments, decisions or activities was the one that felt like too much, but here I sit, dreading today and wondering how I am going to get through it all.

The joy I felt initially with the kids this morning walked out the door with them. I look around, see the ever-present sink full of dishes and think of everything that needs to be handled today, and I want to curl up and cry.

Since life doesn't always give me the option of crawling back in bed for the day, I go to the one place I know I can find help. I climb up onto my Father's lap, press my face into His shoulder and breathe Him in. Knowing His presence to be my refuge, my safe place, I ask Him to walk this day with me, giving me the strength I need to face it all.

Have you ever had days like that? Where life's expectations feel like too much and you want to hide away from it all?

I love the provision God gives us with this verse, *"Let us then approach God's throne of grace with confidence, so that we may receive mercy and find grace to help us in our time of need"* (Hebrews 4:16).

It is such a reassuring promise that He has the resources we need waiting for us, and yet I find myself slightly unsettled with the first part, contrasting in my mind the grand imagery of His throne room with the simple image of being held in my heavenly Father's arms. The wrestling with the image, though, gives new perspective to moments like this. The arms that hold me so tenderly are in reality the strong arms that hold the universe together.

My Father is the Ruler of the Universe. It sounds a bit crazy to say out loud. Can I really enter into the place where He rules the universe and not only be welcomed but find His love, mercy and grace just waiting for me?

His Spirit challenges me with this truth: He chose to destroy all the barriers that would keep me from being able to rush into His arms by literally tearing apart time and space, setting aside His power to come as a servant, and then to die on my behalf. I am now His daughter, a relationship which sweeps aside formal etiquette.

Is there some hesitation that is holding you back from just running into His arms? Please believe that He will help you when you are overwhelmed and can barely move forward in your day. He truly has moved heaven and earth so that you have a direct path to run straight into His throne room as His beloved daughter to find the grace and mercy you need for this moment. The God of the universe longs to hold you tightly in His arms to carry you through today's challenges.

God's reassurance for me is ...

YOU'RE NOT OUT OF CHANCES

ANDREA KETTERING

"You heard me when I cried, 'Listen to my pleading! Hear my cry for help!'
Yes, you came when I called; you told me, 'Do not fear.'"
Lamentations 3:56-57 (NLT)

Slumped at my desk in the human resources department, I dreamed of quitting. I watched as people around me complained about their work, gossiped and fought with co-workers. I observed strong women, some of whom were my mentors, put their work and ambition ahead of their health, family and happiness. All this left me tired, weary and questioning my life's purpose.

Being in my mid-thirties with three young kids and a husband who had recently started his own company meant a lot of expenses coming in with little to no guarantee of income. These stresses, along with a prevailing depression that kept creeping into my heart, started to get the best of me. I could no longer ignore it all. Showing up to work became daunting, and a haunting question kept playing in my head over and over again:

What is my purpose?

I had worked for years to get this job and yet I couldn't stand it. Fear trickled in as I realized my life's plan was not working out and change seemed imminent. I questioned myself incessantly: Wasn't it too late? How could I start over again? Would God give me another chance to get it right?

Day after day, I carried the heaviness that came with having no clear answers. Emotionally drained, I broke down and pleaded with God to help me, to radically change my life, to affirm my purpose. I was like Jeremiah in the book of Lamentations:

"You heard me when I cried, 'Listen to my pleading! Hear my cry for help!' Yes, you came when I called; you told me, Do not fear'" (Lamentations 3:56-57).

Jeremiah was writing to the exiled people of Judah. These people had turned their backs on God and consequently, were tragically living their lives full of fear and stress. In this part of the book, Jeremiah pointed to the time when he was thrown into an empty cistern and left to die. Yet, when he called, God came and rescued him. Jeremiah used this story to impress on the exiles that no matter the circumstances, God is a God of second chances. If you turn to Him, He will rescue you from your stress and fear.

The World Health Organization states that "Stress is the health epidemic of the 21st century." We know stress is a problem, but some may not know stress is caused by an underlying fear. Therefore, if we want to get a handle on our stress, we must pause and ask ourselves, *What is this really about? What am I fearing?* For me, the stress and fear didn't stem from being in a job that I didn't like. It was from living counter to God's purpose for my life.

Not long after my plea with God, I got an email from my boss; the company was trying to reduce employee redundancy due to a recent merger and was offering a compensation package for anyone who wanted to quit. I knew God was opening a door. After lengthy discussions with my husband, I took a leap of faith and quit. I had many fears around our finances and finding another job, but missing out on God's purpose for my life trumped them all.

After months of reflection and prayer, God pointed me in a direction that I'd been running away from ever since my fierce independence declared I would never follow in my parents' footsteps. Ironically, God used my mom to gently ask me, "What about teaching?"

Over the next two years, God consistently confirmed my calling to become a teacher by opening doors I didn't think could be opened. Now, a few weeks away from graduation, I am humbled and filled with a joyful peace knowing that God didn't give up on me, and I am right where I am supposed to be.

Identify your fears, lay them down before God, and rest in His truth that He will rescue you. Don't fear or worry about what lies around the corner because God is already there willing to give you a second chance.

God's reassurance for me is ...

SIX WORDS THAT CHANGED MY LIFE

MARY BOSWELL

"Give us today our daily bread."
Matthew 6:11 (NIV)

Alone. Frustrated. Angry. Hurt. Exhausted. Overwhelmed.

As I sat alone in my car, struggling with questions yet unanswered, those words consumed my mind and soul.

Why did someone I care deeply about fail me?
Why were we still struggling with unmet financial needs?
How was I going to salvage a relationship that was at the breaking point?

In that moment, God interrupted my "pity party for one" to share from His heart to mine the six words that changed my life, making the first six I mentioned irrelevant:

"Give us today our daily bread" (Matthew 6:11).

These six simple words found in Jesus' prayer in Matthew 6:9-13 echoed through my mind. As I sought to understand why God brought this verse to my mind, I came to this realization:

I'd been looking to things and people other than God to fulfill my needs. As a result, I'd become consumed by worry, anxiety and stress over those unmet needs.

Nothing and no one other than God can fulfill my needs. He gives me my daily bread as He sustains me with both my physical and spiritual nourishment for each day.

In this passage, "daily" is the Greek word *epiousion*, which means "sufficient for today."
Deuteronomy 8:3 tells us, *"He humbled you, causing you to hunger and then feeding you with manna ... to teach you that man does not live on bread alone but on every word that comes from the mouth of the LORD"* (NIV).
Our heavenly Father desires to give us both our physical and spiritual nourishment each day.

Stepping out of my car that evening, I committed to focus on Him each morning before anything else. I confessed my lack of focus and committed to trusting Him to meet my needs. I decided to ask my heavenly Father each day to give me exactly what I need for the day. Nothing more. Nothing less.

Now, first thing each morning, before placing one foot on the floor, I ask God to give me His daily manna of strength, peace and comfort (whatever I need both physically and spiritually) to make it through the day.

Then, I spend time in God's Word. These first few minutes of my day spent praying and reading God's Word prepare my heart and mind to receive His daily bread both physically and spiritually.

Do I always get it right? No! But, with each passing day that I start my morning with the prayer, "Lord, give me Your daily bread," I'm prepared to receive His physical and spiritual manna.

Friend, can I ask you something? Do you look to someone or something else to fulfill your needs? Are you consumed by the first six words I mentioned — alone, frustrated, angry, hurt, exhausted and overwhelmed?

Instead of looking to someone or something else, let's allow these six simple words to change our lives. Let's commit to this daily prayer and trust God to give us our daily bread.

God's reassurance for me is ...

FINDING COMFORT IN TIGHT PLACES

COLLENE BORCHARDT

"This is my comfort in my affliction, that your promise gives me life."
Psalm 119:50 (ESV)

The plastic tube for the MRI machine seemed really small as I walked over and laid down on the cold table. The nurse started to push me in, and all I could see were the hard, plastic walls that seemed to be just inches from my face. My breath quickened as the walls seemed to close in on me, my claustrophobia kicking in. My heart raced and tears streamed down my face as I yelled out, "I CAN'T DO THIS!"

The nurse pulled me back out, gave me a minute to compose myself, and then told me we were going to try something. She took a small washcloth and placed it over my eyes.

The washcloth prevented me from seeing the ominous plastic walls around me. It made it so the only way I could see was by looking down my body and out of the tube. And because I could see the way out, I found comfort even in that tight place. My body relaxed, and I was able to endure the test that needed to be done in order for me to move forward, heal and grow.

In the same way, life can shove us into tense circumstances. We sometimes find ourselves stuck between a rock and a hard place. The stress and tensions of life close in on us as the ominous worries fill our mind with fear. Our hearts ache, tears flow down our faces, and we feel like we just can't do this.

But like the nurse who gave me a tactic for enduring an MRI, the Lord has also given us a strategy for surviving the pressing conditions in life. In Psalm 119:50, the Bible says, *"This is my comfort in my affliction, that your promise gives me life."*

The promise the psalmist referred to was God's Word. In His Word, God promises to love us unconditionally. He promises to always be there for us. And He promises to always hear our prayers. Just like the washcloth, those promises can direct our spiritual eyes. That way, instead of looking at the pressures of life surrounding us, we can look only upon the One who has provided a way out.

The stress of our problems may not go away, just as the MRI tube didn't go away for me. But as long as we keep our eyes fixed on Him, we can remain calm and find reassurance in the fact that we will get out eventually. And we can trust that God will work it all out for our good (Romans 8:28), to help us move forward, to help us heal and to help us grow.

When you find yourself in a tight place, remember that God is your comfort in your afflictions, and His promises will give you life. When fear closes in on you and tears blind your eyes, may you find comfort in the One who never leaves your side.

God's reassurance for me is ...

SHE BELIEVED

JENNIFER WILLIAMS

"She believed that God would keep his promise."
Hebrews 11:11b (NLT)

When I was a little girl, my dad raised beagles. Those furry little guys could get a whiff of a rabbit and be on a trail, zigging and zagging forever.

A lot like my mind. It takes just a whiff of something to start my thoughts zigging and zagging. Worrying and stressing down all the big and small rabbit trails. "What if" worries and worst-case scenarios from just a whiff. Even more so in the middle of a mess.

My dad had a whistle that stopped his dogs in their tracks. When he whistled, they not only stopped chasing the rabbit trail, *but they returned to him.*

Worry — a thorn in my side. Picked up on one of those rabbit trails through a briar patch, no doubt. Like a thorn, worry persistently nags at me. However, over the last few years, when my thoughts have started down a rabbit trail, God has specifically been teaching me to trust Him instead. In fact, God even gave me a whistle in Hebrews 11:11 — *a reminder to return my thoughts to Him, to the truth of His Word.*

"She believed that God would keep his promise" (Hebrews 11:11). These words jumped off the pages and straight into my heart. It was like God said, "Do you really believe My promises?" She believed! She, as in Sarah, Abraham's wife, who was old as dirt by this time. Far past childbearing years.

She believed God would keep His promise to give her a son and be the mother of nations. Let's not forget, however, that belief was not her first response.

At first, Sarah laughed. I can hear her now. "Ha! Really? You have got to be joking, God. Did You forget how old we are? I mean just look at me! I am almost 100 years old."

Just like Sarah, we doubt God. We may laugh or cry at our circumstances. We forget to believe God's promises; we forget to think on truth. We worry and fear when we should believe.

Trials. Tribulation. Distress. Frustration. It's inevitable in this world — Jesus said so. (John 16:33) That's why we need to build a firm foundation of trust in God even when we can't see past our circumstances or emotions at the moment.

How do we start? By spending time in His Word daily. God's Word is jam-packed with promises to forgive and redeem us, love us, never leave us, provide for us, direct us, protect us, comfort us and give us hope. Discover His promises for your life! Write them on your heart. Find your whistle.

Like Sarah, we must consciously stop going down that rabbit trail of worry and unbelief. We must learn to listen to the whistle, stop worry in its tracks and believe that God will keep His promises. Really believe! *"Let us hold unswervingly to the hope we profess, for he who promised is faithful"* (Hebrews 10:23, NIV).

God's reassurance for me is ...

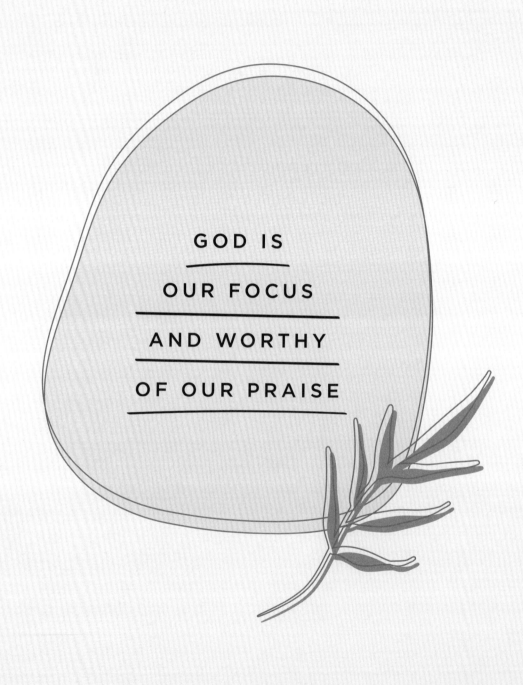

GOD IS

OUR FOCUS

AND WORTHY

OF OUR PRAISE

HOW TO FIGHT BACK WHEN FEAR WAGES WAR

KAITLIN GARRISON

"And let the peace of Christ rule in your hearts, to which indeed you were called in one body. And be thankful. Let the word of Christ dwell in you richly, teaching and admonishing one another in all wisdom, ..."
Colossians 3:15-16a (ESV)

The battle began the moment I opened my eyes. Morning after morning, feelings of dread and anxiety invaded my mind. I was in the thick of my first year of teaching and no matter how hard I tried, I couldn't find relief from anxiety.

I kept reminding myself, *Fear is a liar.* But its response was so loud: *Things will always be this way; you will always feel this way.* Day after day, I was the victim of a battle I couldn't see and felt powerless to win.

New seasons of life can fuel anxiety because we're unsure of the unknown and feel incompetent in navigating new waters. Any kind of change tends to challenge our comfort zone and cause us to question who we are and what we're capable of. Thankfully, in his letter to the church at Colossae, Paul gives us a three-step battle plan that reminds us of our identity in Christ and can help us fight fear, especially in the midst of uncharted waters:

" And let the peace of Christ rule in your hearts, to which indeed you were called in one body. And be thankful. Let the word of Christ dwell in you richly, teaching and admonishing one another in all wisdom, ..." (Colossians 3:15-16).

1. *"Let the peace of Christ rule ..."*
The Greek word used for rule is *brabeuō* meaning "to be an umpire." Umpires always have the last word. When we let the peace of Christ be the "umpire" in our hearts, we cling to Gospel truths that bring us peace and reject the lies. For me, this looks like carrying around a "battle book" filled with verses that target anxiety. Reading these verses out loud puts both fear and God in their rightful place.

2. *" And be thankful ..."*
Recently, scientists have released research showing the impact thankfulness has on diminishing stress and worry. When we are in a state of anxiety, we see all the places we are lacking. However, when we thank God for even the smallest things, we acknowledge the abundance in our story. It is harder for anxiety to cloud our vision when we are frequently acknowledging the provision of God throughout our day.

3. *" Admonishing each other in all wisdom ..."*
God has graciously given us the body of believers who possess different strengths and gifts. During those fear-ridden mornings, I would call or text a friend, and they would pray for me, encourage me or send me a word of wisdom that carried me through my day. It's a beautiful thing to invite your tribe into your struggle and watch God fight for you through them.

Friend, the Lord has equipped us to fight fear through His Word, the body of believers and through the power of Christ in us. Though anxiety may wage war for control of our minds, we can call on the name of the Prince of Peace who silences every fear.

God's reassurance for me is ...

A SPIRIT OF THANKSGIVING

MANDY JOHNSON

"Rejoice always, pray continually, give thanks in all circumstances;
for this is God's will for you in Christ Jesus."
1 Thessalonians 5:16-18 (NIV)

This was one of those days. My to-do list was long enough to wrap around a shopping mall, and I needed to get moving if anything was going to be accomplished in the short window of time available. I raced out of the house to begin my errands, aiming to be the hero of the day who picked up dry-cleaning, purchased everyone's favorite groceries and cooked a hot meal by dinner time.

Then the frustration started ...

Why do people drive under the speed limit? Can that person please use their blinker? Get out of my way! I don't have time for this.

I felt the tension in my chest start to rise at each twist and turn down the road. My own expectations piled on pressure until it finally consumed me: the crippling weight of anxiety. My attitude, personality and ability to think reasonably diminished. I pulled into a parking lot to breathe, and felt the Holy Spirit gently remind me of the words we read in 1 Thessalonians 5:16-18: *"Rejoice always, pray continually, give thanks in all circumstances; for this is God's will for you in Christ Jesus."*

Candidly, the last thing on my mind while feeling anxious is to rejoice or express gratitude. I'd much rather hide, try to sort everything out on my own or eat a sleeve of Oreo cookies. I definitely don't feel grateful. But Paul's words are guiding lights to fix our hearts and minds upon whether we are in stress or not.

God's will for us is to rejoice out of obedience, to pray and to give thanks to our heavenly Father who deeply cares. God enters into our anxious moments with us, ready and armed to go to battle on our behalf. He is our stable source of comfort when we feel unequipped and overwhelmed.

As I continued to gather myself, I took a deep breath and began to make a mental list of what I was grateful for in that moment: My family. My health. The ability to breathe. Jesus.

My heart rate dropped, my shoulders lowered. Anxiety makes the most important things in life seem small, and the small things in life seem most important. But gratitude, fueled by faith, helps us slowly come back to life. Even when we don't feel an ounce of gratitude in our bones, there is always something to be grateful for. When we are grateful, we are in God's will.

We all have lengthy to-do lists, but it's how we complete them that matters to God. Are we relying on our own strength or are we led by a spirit of thanksgiving?

God's reassurance for me is ...

KEEPING OUR MINDS IN PERFECT PEACE

SARAH E. BROOKS

"You keep him in perfect peace whose mind is stayed on you, because he trusts in you."
Isaiah 26:3 (ESV)

I used to be fearless. Now, I was so afraid I could barely breathe. I wiped my tears with my sleeve and struggled to slow my ragged breathing. My heart continued racing as I ended the call with the doctor's office.

My 5-month-old played happily on the floor — completely oblivious to the situation we were facing. In two weeks, I would hand her over to a pediatric neurosurgeon for her first brain surgery. A genetic defect meant that my daughter's life was at risk, and emergency brain surgery was the only solution.

I felt hopeless.
I felt anxious.

The future was no longer something to look forward to but something to fear.

My mind focused on all the things that could go wrong. What if she suffered brain damage? What if the surgery fails? What if I lose her?

Each "what if" led me further down a hole of anxiety and fear. The more I focused on my problem, the more worry wove its way into my heart. It was a fear that felt tangible.

The night before her surgery, I begged for God's peace and protection. I wanted Him to promise me that everything was going to be OK. I looked over to where my daughter slept soundly in her bassinet. She smiled and sighed in her sleep. She wasn't worried about tomorrow. God brought to mind the words I had read earlier that day in Isaiah 26:3: "*You keep him in perfect peace whose mind is stayed on you, because he trusts in you.*" In that moment, I felt God whisper, "Do you trust Me?"

God didn't promise me the surgery would be successful. He didn't promise that all my problems would be solved in an instant, but He reminded me that He is trustworthy. Even if my greatest fears came true, He would be with me every step of the way.

Peace comes not when our problems disappear but when we choose to fix our hearts and minds on who God is. He is the keeper of our peace. When I focus on my problems, I worry. When I focus on my God, I experience His peace and presence. It's a daily, minute-by-minute choice to focus my mind on Him.

Peace comes when we learn to fix our hearts, eyes and minds not on our situation but on our Savior. As we learn to trust, we learn that He is trustworthy. A mind kept "in perfect peace" will be able to endure life's storms, because she trusts the one who is in control of the waves.

God's reassurance for me is ...

CHOOSING STILLNESS IN THE PRESENCE OF ANXIETY

DIANE BROOKS

"Be still, and know that I am God; ..."
Psalm 46:10 (NIV)

The weatherman said a storm was coming. I think there was one already brewing in my body. From the moment I wrote the impossible-to-accomplish list, my heart was pounding and wild thoughts were spinning in my mind. I had let my focus shift from God's goodness to my ability, and questions lingered as to how I was going to get everything done.

I had been up before dawn racing room to room cleaning before company arrived and my troubling anxiety had hit high gear, consuming me. As I dashed past the sunroom, the most spectacular purplish-pink light rested along the cloud line, catching my eyes. It beckoned me, inviting me to sit, and I did.

Over the next few minutes, the sky gave way to the bright yellow sunrise, and I began to whisper the beginning of my favorite verse: *"Be still and know I am God; ..."* (Psalm 46:10). With every inhale, I told myself to be still, and on the exhale, I repeated everything I could remember of God.

Be still and know God is my Refuge.
Be still and know God is my Strength.
Be still and know God is my Rock.
Be still and know God is my Deliverer.

Be still — and then the clouds swallowed the sun's rising color. In the small space of time, I realized my anxious heart had become calm and the busy thoughts no longer raced within me. Stunned by the beauty, I praised God for His goodness.

In the midst of mind-spinning, heart-thumping, "body going so fast it's about to crash" anxiety, God had created a moment, offered an opportunity, and I followed, choosing stillness in the presence of anxiety.

Rather than return to the cleaning race, I decided to read God's Word: *"God is our refuge and strength, a very present help in trouble. Therefore we will not fear ... The LORD of hosts is with us; the God of Jacob is our fortress. Selah. Come, behold the works of the LORD ... Be still, and know that I am God. I will be exalted among the nations, I will be exalted in the earth!"* (Psalm 46:1, 2a, 7-8, 10, ESV)

God is our present help. He invites us to notice Him, to set aside all that weighs heavy, to cease striving after all that consumes, and know Him. God wants us to understand He is with us and for us; we do not need to fear. Isn't this the root of our anxiety? When our fear for God is replaced with fears in the world?

God promises He will be exalted. To do this, we must Selah — we must pause to seek Him in order to acknowledge who He is. God requires us to be still and know Him first. Stop and behold God, look and understand His goodness, and contemplate Him with joy overflowing. Then we will not be able to contain ourselves! We will exalt God, and our anxiety will fade as we focus on Him.

God's reassurance for me is ...

THE GIFT OF GRAY AREAS

JANET KHOKHAR

"And now, Lord, what do I wait for? My hope is in You."
Psalm 39:7 (NKJV)

Bright banners in primary colors and the sharp scent of crayon wax belied the heavy atmosphere around the conference table. Six school administrators and the county's senior psychologist eyed me sympathetically.

"So you're saying that even if Luke didn't have autism, he still has an intellectual disorder?" I asked, my stomach tightening.

"Yes, that's right." The psychologist smoothed his hand over the cognitive evaluation that showed just how low my son scored compared to typical students. "Although Luke's autism may be on the severe side, he also has an intellectual disability that would qualify him for services."

Services, as in moving Luke off a high school diploma track and into a non-degree track life skills program. College was out. In truth, it was never on the list of possibilities.

And a list was what I hoped for. A plan from God. A 1-2-3 guarantee. The solidarity of certainty.

Maybe you've hoped to uproot uncertainty, too. If only we could take a test, read the right book, or hear the Holy Spirit declare, "Now, this is what you need to do," then our anxieties would vanish. But as I drove away from the school, grieving the gray areas that whitewashed my son's future in mystery, I remembered something.

God did His greatest work in me through the gray areas of uncertainty.

When I stumbled forward, one step at a time, seeing little ahead, I relied on other senses. My hearing came alive as I listened to that still, small voice before I retorted in anger. My hands put down my phone and picked up a Bible. My lips learned to say "Change me, Lord" before "Fix my husband." I locked my eyes on God, believing that where I fixed my eyes, my feet would follow.

In the gray areas, I grew.

King David also learned to navigate the gray areas by fixing his eyes on God. In Psalm 39:7, David wrote, *"And now, Lord, what do I wait for? My hope is in You."*

Fraught with enemies on his borders and in his household, David had few guarantees. But he knew that the gray areas of uncertainty weren't unknown to God. When would David stop running from Saul and ascend the throne? Would he be vindicated from the slander of a once-dear friend? Although David didn't know the future, he did know its Author. And there David fixed his eyes. He trusted his unseen future to an all-seeing God, and so can we.

You may be struggling to see beyond the gray mist of a broken marriage or perilous financial stress or, like me, wrestling with a child's unknown future, but we can take comfort in the guarantees of God:

I don't need to know everything — I need God.
I don't need every step laid before me — I need to take the first step.
I don't need certainty — I need confidence in an unshakable God.

Our only guarantee is God, and the only fixed point is found in Christ. And where our eyes are fixed, our feet will follow. This is the gift of gray areas.

God's reassurance for me is ...

Acknolwledments

Proverbs 31 Ministries and COMPEL Training would like to offer a special thanks to the talented devotion writers featured in this book, all of whom are members of COMPEL Training. Their devotions were chosen out of over 600 submissions in a COMPEL devotion writing challenge. Writers, we congratulate and applaud you for your hard work and dedication to your craft of writing, and for bravely offering your words of truth and encouragement to the world. You are touching hearts and lives in ways you will never understand until eternity. Keep up the good work, faithful servants!

"Therefore, since we are surrounded by such a great cloud of witnesses, let us throw off everything that hinders and the sin that so easily entangles. And let us run with perseverance the race marked out for us, fixing our eyes on Jesus, the pioneer and perfecter of faith. For the joy set before him he endured the cross, scorning its shame, and sat down at the right hand of the throne of God. Consider him who endured such opposition from sinners, so that you will not grow weary and lose heart." Hebrews 12:1-3 (NIV)

Notes

Know the Truth. Live the Truth. It changes everything.

If you were inspired by this devotion and desire to deepen your own personal relationship with Jesus Christ, Proverbs 31 Ministries has just what you are looking for.

Proverbs 31 Ministries exists to be a trusted friend who will take you by the hand and walk by your side, leading you one step closer to the heart of God through:

- Free online daily devotions.

- First 5 Bible study app.

- Online Bible Studies.

- Proverbs 31 Podcast.

- COMPEL Training.

- She Speaks Conference.

- Books and resources.

Our desire is to help you to know the Truth and live the Truth.
Because when you do, it changes everything.

For more information about Proverbs 31 Ministries, visit: **proverbs31.org.**

Proverbs 31
MINISTRIES

COMPEL TRAINING

COMPEL Training is a faith-based online training community designed to help writers find direction for their work, receive practical training and discover the motivation to keep going.

We've built COMPEL around three pillars:

COMMUNITY – with other writers and COMPEL leaders.

CONTENT – that is practical and inspiring.

CONNECTION – with experts in their field and writing opportunities.

Sign-up for just $30/month at

compeltraining.com.

encouragement for today

DAILY DEVOTIONS

WHAT DOES THE BIBLE SAY ABOUT WHAT YOU'RE GOING THROUGH?

SUBSCRIBE TO OUR FREE *ENCOURAGEMENT FOR TODAY* DAILY DEVOTIONS TO RECEIVE DAILY, BIBLICAL ENCOURAGEMENT THAT WILL HELP YOU FILTER EVERYDAY LIFE THROUGH THE TRUTH OF GOD'S WORD.

Go to www.proverbs31.org/devotions to sign up for free!

> *We must exchange whispers with God before shouts with the world.*

THE
FIRST 5 MOBILE APP!

Designed for you to spend the first five minutes of your day reading and studying God's Word.

This free mobile app will take you through the Bible chapter by chapter, with daily teachings and weekend audio recordings to accompany each passage of Scripture.

DOWNLOAD
from your smartphone app store!

WWW.FIRST5.ORG